Waiting to Bloom

KATHLEEN M. HOLDEN

ISBN 978-1-64140-726-7 (paperback)
ISBN 978-1-64140-727-4 (digital)

Christian Faith Publishing, Inc.
832 Park Avenue
Meadville, PA 16335
www.christianfaithpublishing.com

Printed in the United States of America

Contents

But as for me and my household,
    we will serve the Lord.
        —Joshua 24:15

Chapter 1

O ne of my earliest memories takes me back to the second grade: my mom lovingly stitching and fitting me for the gown that I would wear to my first Holy Communion (a sacramental ritual practiced in the Catholic faith). Other memories include playing in the backyard with my siblings, participating in activities at the swim club that our family had membership in, and long trips on family vacations. Life was pretty good as far as my early memories can recall.

I grew up in what I would consider a close-knit, traditional Catholic family where my parents enforced following the guidelines of the Catholic Church appropriately. We attended mass regularly, learned and recited all of the standard Catholic prayers, and lived out the annual rituals of confession, communion, baptism, confirmation, and the other rites of passage Catholics are to follow. My father, years before I was born, had actually practiced the Methodist religion until he met my mother. According to Catholic guidelines, to officially be married in the church, both parties had to be followers in Catholic beliefs, and agree to practice and raise their future children according to the Catholic faith. My father was a man devoted to his family. With desire to accommodate the Catholic view, he studied the Catholic ways and converted to Catholicism in order to marry my mother. I love and respect my parents deeply, yet I find it amusing that you can simply take the right steps, follow the man-made guidelines, and transfer into a new religion that better suits personal needs. Ironically, I made a similar decision later in my life when I transferred out of the Catholic religion and into the Lutheran religion. It was a mere legality of the faith, and I was willing to abide by the guidelines of that religion to accommodate my situational circumstance. I knew in my heart that I believed in God and that God was leading my life. I found that in both the Catholic religion and the Lutheran religion, I would be following those same beliefs; the title of Catholic or Lutheran meant nothing to me. My parents had been amazing role models and had taught me well. The life lesson I took from them was simple: faith was important. I assumed that as long as I had some kind of faith based on the Bible, I was doing well (on the spiritual end of life).

In our home, faith surrounded much of our lives. As infants, our parents had us baptized in the Catholic Church, and we attended masses weekly. As we approached school age, we were sent for private Catholic education, and the excitement built as we reached the milestone of second grade, where we were prepared to receive our first Holy Communion. This is the memory I have of my mom: making my white eyelet dress with the cascading veil. As we continued to grow up in the faith, I recall when my brothers were taught to serve as altar boys as they reached the appropriate ages. Not only did we follow the strict Catholic guidelines and meet every ritual, but during my elementary years, my mom was also quite active in our church and school. The payoff of having such strong interactions within the church was the great number of friendships my parents had acquired over the years. Our home was a strong and loving environment. We worked together and played together well in those early elementary years of my memory.

My family's downward spiral hit during my middle school years, with a cancer diagnosis for my father. This was not the first battle our family had faced against this wretched disease. My mother had experienced a battle with Hodgkin's lymphoma when I was young—so young that I do not remember her battle, but only the discussion of it when the topic came up. After Mom had fought and won her battle, she was faced with the heartache of explaining to four young children what new battle lay ahead for us. It was no surprise that she turned to the church to find support in how to handle presenting this news. Because of her involvement in our education, it was easy for her to gather immediate support when this difficult time came.

On a wintery afternoon in March, my siblings and I were called to the school office where Mom had gathered with the principal and church priest. Joined in a circle, Mom proceeded to tell us of how our father had collapsed earlier that morning while they were attending church services together. She went on to explain that they had spent the day at the hospital, where my father remained. She informed us that the tests concluded that dad had a brain tumor and this is what had caused his body to give out. We were told that he was resting in the hospital and that surgery would soon follow to remove the tumor on his brain. She provided more details and mentioned the word *cancer* but I was uncertain of how to process everything that I was hearing. As a young child, I took in what I could from that meeting: my dad was sick, but the doctors were going to make him well.

My dad was a quiet, well-educated, and respected man with a heart for serving others. I do not know all of the details of his life, but I know that he had faced his share of struggles. As a young boy, my father lost his only brother in a house fire when they were quite small, and later, he had lost his first wife in an automobile accident. This left him with two grown children who later became my half brother and half sister. He became a parent the second time around when he married my mother years later. As an older parent, he had already reached the age of retirement when I was beginning my elementary school years. His career as an engineer transitioned postretirement into serving our community in various fixer-upper projects and community service. He had also taken a part-time job at a local hardware store simply because he enjoyed staying busy. He loved having time to work in his oversized garden and his self-constructed greenhouse, which were both located near the back of our family property. I loved spending time with Dad in the garden and the greenhouse, but my favorite memories with my dad were of me curled up on the couch resting on his chest. He would sit quietly, almost motionless, and I would lay my head on his chest and listen to his heartbeat. I would ask him silly elementary questions, and he would answer in his quiet, confident voice. If I truly sit back and reflect on those memories, I can recall his gentle chuckle as I would say something that made him giddy. His past had made him a fighter who was always ready to conquer any hurdle, yet as fierce as he had to be in difficulty, his core was gentle and loving. I was always proud to be Daddy's little girl.

Being older but in excellent health overall, his surgery and treatment began within days of our family meeting. I remember having many questions but not knowing how or when to ask them. The hardest part for me was coming home each day after school to find another day passing with my dad still being hospitalized. I didn't understand the disease, so I could not understand the treatment. As each day passed, I longed for my daddy. It seemed like I had to wait an eternity, but finally we were able to visit him at the hospital. As we entered his room, Dad greeted us with the same calm, gentle disposition he always carried. He hugged each one of the kids and gave Mom the traditional kiss they always exchanged. The visit was full of excitement, and I remember bombarding Dad with a variety of questions and talking about things going on in school and with our sports. Although we were giddy and delighted to see Dad, he could tell that we were also nervous and afraid. His sleek, confident appearance had now been situationally altered with a massive black eye and an extensive white bandage covering his head. To lighten the fear, Dad told us of how he was now (post-surgery) able to do magic. He told us that he was able to raise his eyebrows individually instead of raising both together as most people do. With all of our attention focused on Dad, he smiled and speedily raised one eyebrow and then quickly shifted and raised the other one completely independent of each-other. We giggled hysterically as our dad continued to entertain us with his new skill. His eyebrows now looked like two caterpillars chasing after one another in a race that neither one would win. Dad went on to explain that while they were in surgery, a nerve was cut, which now allowed him to perform this way. It was the perfect way to lessen our fears and enjoy the time we had with our dad during his recovery. Although he brought much laughter to us during that visit, we eventually had to leave him. When it was my turn to say goodbye, I climbed up on his lap and wrapped my arms tightly around his neck. I did not want to be separated from my dad again. I was glad that I had had my time with him, but I wanted him to come home with me. Eventually, I was pulled away from my dad that night, but fortunately, I did not have to wait too long to find my joy again. Soon after that visit, Dad was strong enough to return home once again where I could hug him and sit with him as often as I desired, and I made sure I did just that.

After Dad's return home, we attempted to return to life as we had previously known it. We continued with our schooling and our social activities. Mom sought help from other parents for carpooling and other needs, but overall, life seemed happy. The biggest change was Dad's hectic schedule with doctor visits and hospital runs, but Mom managed to maintain those commitments while we were at school. Although she tried to keep our lives as normal as possible, there were many things that created concern and question in my mind. But just as I had done the day we first learned of his illness, I kept it all in. I was just a child. I did not know how to take all of my thoughts and feelings and compile them correctly to form appropriate questions or have meaningful conversations. Instead, I maintained the role of being Daddy's little girl. What that meant to me was simply to check on Dad after his appointments and give him as many hugs as I could. I managed that role well.

I followed up every appointment (that I was aware of) by asking Dad what the doctor had said. I honestly cannot recall what he told me each time, nor do I think I really understood. I think I truly was asking because my question gave me a reason to crawl up on his lap for at least a few minutes of his undivided attention. In all of the days that I remember checking in on him, it was my last check-in that I will never forget.

I remember sitting on an afternoon bus ride, eagerly waiting to get into our neighborhood. I knew dad had gone to the doctor that day, and as my routine had established, I couldn't wait to jump in his lap and find out what the doctor had said. As the bus approached our house, I grabbed my schoolbag and waited for the door to open. As it did, I ran down the steps, up the long driveway, and through the door into the house. I found Dad resting quietly in his recliner, and while I was still running up to him, I asked what the doctor had said. I remember beginning to climb over the arm of the chair as I always did, eagerly waiting for both his verbal response, as well as his loving arms to embrace me, but that day was different. My climb was interrupted midway as it was my mom's arms that scooped me up and placed me in a standing position next to my dad's chair. She proceeded to tell me that, according to the doctors, Dad didn't need medicine anymore. I remember feeling elated! I knew my dad was a fighter. From the very beginning, I knew that Dad was going to get better, and that was just what I heard my mom saying that day. I had lived so many months with questions and emotions that I was forced to keep inside, but those concerns didn't matter anymore. As far as I understood, my dad was over his illness, and I was able to let go of those worries.

During the next few weeks, my dad's schedule continued with his doctor appointments, but I didn't follow them as I had done before. I continued to hear Mom and Dad discussing health issues, but the weight of my concern and confusion had lessened greatly. Medical conversations, from the time I was very young, were common in my home because of my mother's previous battle. In addition to my mom's history of lymphoma, I heard reference to medical concerns regarding my half sister, Carol Ann, for most of my early life as well. Although she was quite a bit older than I and lived outside of our home, I was aware that throughout her life, she had struggled with various medical illnesses, one being a battle with leukemia. Her battle happened to fall simultaneously with my dad's cancer battle. As I continued to hear vague medical conversations around the house, I found comfort in reflecting on my mom's earlier words. I had come to the conclusion that Dad was doing well, so even with these ongoing conversations, I was not concerned about my dad.

As that year progressed, I noticed my dad continuing to change. His balding head, more frequent wheelchair use, and fewer and fewer father-daughter conversations ignited a new concern in my heart; however, I was instructed by Mom to continue on with my normal activities. Trusting her leadership, I obeyed her request. I began attending most soccer games with teammates, and family outings grew less often. I remember being confused, but again, I could find no way to compile my thoughts to ask questions or express concerns. I kept it all to myself and held fast to my conclusion that Dad was getting better.

Eventually, my curiosity got the best of me, and I found myself creeping around listening to conversations that I probably should not have been. One particular night, I heard my mom and dad in the kitchen. I snuck down the hall and stayed hidden behind some furniture. I listened very quietly as my dad's voice was almost inaudible. The one phrase I head very clearly was, "If I lose her, it will kill me." My confusion reached a new height as I had no idea what they had been talking about. I simply knew that my dad was extremely upset. I snuck back down the hall, having achieved my goal of not being seen. I took those words away with me and again held them in with many questions left unanswered.

Unfortunately, the mystery soon solved itself. My next memory is sitting beside my dad at the funeral home where we laid Carol Ann to rest. My once strong, confident, hero, was now wheelchair bound and weak. As the funeral commenced, my heart broke as I looked over at my dad, only to see endless tears falling from his eyes. In that moment, I saw an entirely new person—once a fighter, but now left speechless, broken, and defeated. I could not begin to understand the depth of pain that he experienced on that day. My dad was a fighter and a man of his word. He had always put his family first, and the church was a central part of his success. During his battle, he continued to grow stronger in his faith as his body weakened, but the pain of this loss stole the last bit of his physical strength. Less than three months after burying his oldest daughter, my dad gave up on his battle against cancer as well.

For you have been my refuge,
a strong tower against the foe
—Psalms 60:3

Chapter 2

O ver the next few months, my mom was forced to plan a funeral, take on the financial burdens of the family, and learn how to become a single mother, but she did not find herself doing it alone. The church, which she had dedicated her life and family to, had appropriately stepped in and provided support in every way. Although my mom was a fighter and was actively doing many things on her own, she was blessed also through financial offerings, meal preparations, and much comfort and support through various visits from friends and members of the church. The outpouring of love that came to us as a family unit was absolutely wonderful; however, personally, I was longing for anyone to notice my pain. As each measure of support came along, I greeted the experience with a smile and gratitude; however, inside I was falling apart. Emotionally, I was closing myself off. As friends came to check in with Mom, I would politely step back and find myself hiding in the quietness of my room. The many hours I spent in there alone gave me time to ponder my pain. I was daddy's girl and had watched him give in to a devastating and difficult battle. I was left alone to process the pain and expected to pick up the pieces of my broken heart on my own.

Through no fault of her own and unequipped in the knowledge of the progression of grief in children, my mom and her friends encouraged me to continue with my childhood activities. As I had always done, I obeyed her requests. As I internally worked through my grief alone, I began to rationalize what had happened previously, during my dad's battle. I realized that during his decline, although I was obediently participating in my activities, more importantly, I was missing precious time with my father. Time that I was beginning to recognize as moments *she* had stolen from me by pushing me toward soccer, piano, and other activities. It was not until after his passing, in my many hours of being alone, that I began to deeply reflect on how much time I actually missed with him. I started to realize how much more time I could have had with my dad, but she stole that from me. As I focused on this day after day, I could feel anger being harvested in my heart, but I kept this bottled up inside as well. As I was moving deeper and deeper into a depression, my mom continued to find strength and support from the church. As she moved forward with her grief and healing, I fell deeper into a world where abandonment and fear fueled my motivations.

As time had passed and routines began to become normal again, I eventually had to return to school. I remember the first day I went back after Dad's funeral. I walked into the classroom and looked around. My feelings of being lonely and abandoned were greatly enhanced when I saw the joy the other kids had. These were the same kids I had been in school with since the beginning of my elementary career. I had gotten to know them well as we learned together, and I had always felt welcomed and a part of our class, but as I stood there that morning, I recognized how different I now was. The emotional withdrawal that I had begun at home was easily set in place at school now as well. I quickly realized that there was not another child in my class who had lived through the losses I had experienced. Although I found myself in a classroom of friends, internally I realized I was all alone.

I showed up to school every day as I was required and participated in class the same as I had prior to my losses, but inside I continued to pull away. Every morning I would get ready for school without my dad, and every day I would return home to find him missing. I needed my daddy, and there was no way to bring him back. I sat through every eight-hour school day pondering over the fact that my mom had lied to me about his illness. I know *now* that it was her effort to protect me, but back then, it did not make any sense to me. She had altered some of the information from the physician and neglected to share the fact that my dad's cancer was incurable. My anger was growing more powerful day by day. I had lost control of the outside world, and I was trying hard to maintain control of the inside. I began using food as a control, which would open the door to many years of struggling through the mental trauma of living with eating disorders. My hidden fear, unrelenting anger and agonizing emotional pain soon took control over me internally as well.

Mentally and emotionally, I was doing everything that I could, just to survive, but the pain continued to build and nag at my core. The methods I had employed to try and reach any level of coping were not enough, the level of hurt within me was beyond measure, and soon I had transitioned beyond mental and emotional strategies and began trying to deal with the pain physically. I had come to a point, unintentionally, where the pain within me was so great, that I had resorted to inflicting physical pain on myself in the form of cutting and burning my skin. I found that this physical pain actually hurt less than the turmoil that was going on within my heart and mind.

I was actively using every method (mentally, emotionally, and now physically) that I could to try and hold myself together, but all of my efforts proved to be in vain. I found that the unyielding agony of living without my dad brought such despair that emotional break downs were still inevitable. It seemed these moments came when I least expected them and instead of bringing relief, these outbursts only brought embarrassment. No one seemed to understand why I would suddenly breakdown, and the events provoking my responses never quite matched. I recall sitting through a slide show presentation at school where one slide triggered a memory of my dad and I absolutely lost it. I could not explain why I was so upset to anyone and felt completely isolated; and that is only one example. Each time I would experience something, I felt more and more cut off from the already lonely life I was living.

Eventually, I decided that tears proved a person's weakness and I was determined to never let anyone see me cry ever again. I learned how to control my breathing when emotion would well up and I also adopted soda as a best friend. I learned that taking deep swallows of the fizzy beverage or intense deep breaths would help me to "push" the emotion down into hidden parts of my soul. I convinced myself that avoiding tears modeled strength and I grew proud knowing that I had learned how to push people away and protect myself from additional hurts.

Although I had a twisted sense of pride in my accomplishments, I continued to self-destruct internally. The issues with food continued as well as the episodes of self-harm. As I lived out these methods of relieving my pain, I found that I still experienced an inability to withdraw from everything. In as much as I could find to do to hold in my grief, I also found myself in explosive outbursts of anger toward my mom. After multiple years of this anger building inside of me, it had altered my mind. I had come to the conclusion that mothers and daughters were not designed to get along. I felt that mothers and daughters were supposed to be enemies. I did not have anything that I could talk to my mom about, and the level of bitterness was high in my heart. The pain in our relationship was so extreme that I actually felt relief when I was able to yell at her at the top of my lungs expressing how much I hated her. I had even gone to the extent of shouting my desire for her to die, right in her face. Month after month, these angry outbursts continued. Each time I could feel the separation in our relationship grow wider and wider. In a twisted way, I felt proud for the division I was causing, and I got joy from the pain I saw that I was putting her through. The anger and pain of my grief became the fuel I needed to survive alone in this world. I did not need anyone, and I was determined to push away anyone who tried to get close to me. Little did I know that my words would come back to haunt me.

Chapter *3*

y high school years did not begin much differently than
my middle school years. Shortly after starting high
school, I was again called to the school office. This time,
I was met only by our school principal and my sister, but the news
was to be expected. In our much smaller meeting, it was confirmed
that our family would once again be facing a battle with cancer, only
this time it was my mother who was facing the battle. So far, our
family had battled leukemia, Hodgkin's lymphoma, and brain cancer. The new battle would be against a well-advanced progression
with colon cancer. Emotionally, I found myself even more confused.
I had learned how to block people out and felt I was "strong" and
successfully living my life "alone," but I was determined not to add
orphan to my growing list of personal titles. Upon the moment of
hearing my mother's diagnosis, I turned a switch internally. Whether
it was fear of another loss or just exhaustion from being depressed
and angry all the time, I was immediately able to turn my anger into
passion. Sitting in the school office that day, I determined, in my
mind, that I would be the one to save my mom. I had decided that I
would be the one to push her through her uphill battle, and together,
we would be the strongest team ever to face cancer and win.

I literally went overnight from hating my mother to being her
number 1 cheerleader. Although I was still young, I accepted the
task of learning her medication routine, knowing her schedule of
procedures, and following her progression just as I had done with

my dad. There were again many people who stepped in to help my mom, which was a necessity as I was not yet able to drive and I had to attend school daily, but I did everything within my power to help her fight her battle. At one point, my mother wrote and presented me with a letter. In the many years of pain and hurt I had caused her, she had every right to fire back with powerful ammunition to even out the pain. However, in that letter, instead of reciprocating the anger and hateful words that I had spoken to her all too many times, my mom wrote that I had become the lifeline that she needed and would continue to need. Her written words broke me to my core and tore down one layer of the emotional shield I had been holding up for so many years. My darkened heart was softened as I read her words and cried through every line she had scripted. She had modeled forgiveness to me in a way I had never experienced. I did not deserve the love and grace she was expressing to me. As a practicing Catholic, I was not familiar with forgiveness outside of the church confessional, where I had been taught to speak my sins to the priest. In those weeks of service to my mom, I received her forgiveness. No special words were needed, nor any priest. She knew of my sorrow and forgave me without any hesitation or penance.

In the weeks and months that followed, I continued to push her, often at times when she physically could do no more. Although still too young to truly understand the disease progression, I was strongly motivated by my passion to make her well. I often reflected on her words that I was her lifeline, and I took that role seriously. I found myself praying for my mom's health to be restored. I continued to spend as much time with Mom as possible, while continuing to pursue my education and plan my future.

Mom, early in her battle, had shared with me that her goal was to beat her illness or at least fight it until all of her children had graduated high school. This was a high goal to achieve as the doctors had originally only given her about six months, from the point of diagnosis, to live. She proved that statistic wrong. She battled her cancer for more than two years, though in the end, she did not fulfill her mission to see each of her children graduate. In each step of her battle, however, her faith never wavered. As I watched her fight, I found myself reflecting on how her faith had been her pillar of strength. She had built a unique foundation where love was vast and support was endless. I was not sure exactly how she had accomplished this, but I was confident that this was a path that I wanted in my life, and God confirmed that in her last days.

As Mom's progression moved into her last two weeks, we went through the expected ups and downs that come with the disease. Through her decline, we converted our living room into a makeshift hospital to better care for her. On the evening of July 17, 1993, my siblings and I were called to her bedside. She had been in a deep sleep for a few days at the time, and we were told by our hospice nurse that we were experiencing the end. It was obvious to us that she was working toward her last breaths, but we did not know exact timing. My siblings and I began a bedside ritual where we could only sit and wait. At times, we would talk with Mom, but most often we would be talking with each other or friends of our mom's who had stopped by. The evening rolled into the late hours of the night, and no one knew exactly what would take place minute by minute. We sat faithfully with Mom, individually as well as a sibling group. Her silence was ongoing yet peaceful.

At one point, without warning, Mom began to speak. It was obvious by her choice of words that she was no longer with us in spirit as she was talking only to people who were not in the room. She called out to these people by name, and we quickly recognized that the names were of family members who had passed before her. During these interactions, we just stood there confused and trying to process her words. We had never experienced anything like this, nor had we really even talked about anything of this nature. We listened to her and tried to put our understanding into the situation. We tried to meet her needs and decipher what she was saying, but reality was that she simply was not in an earthly mindset. As we gained wisdom that this was not a situation that we could manage, we simply stood by her bedside and observed the interactions.

Following this exchange, we continued our bedside ritual. I remained near the foot of her bed on her left side, while my sister stood next to me, near the head of the bed. The early evening hours had passed, and yet we continued to wait, uncertain of the time we had left. At one point in my waiting, my attention was shifted as I felt an extreme, cool peace surround me and pass by me, seeming to flow across her bed toward where my brother was standing on the other side. The peaceful wind that passed was immediately followed by a strong aroma of fresh roses. This unexpected, immediate, and beautifully refreshing scent took my breath away! There was not a single fresh flower in my mom's room, yet the fragrant scent that was filling the air made it seem as if I were standing in an endless rose garden. The only emotion I recall feeling was pure excitement as I immediately grabbed my mom's hand and began to tell her to go with Dad. There was nothing that could explain what was happening except the presence of God, and I did not want my mom to miss her calling. There was no easy explanation for this peaceful breeze as there were no windows in Mom's room open and no fan that could cause the increased movement of air.

The passing of the breeze and floral scent was felt again and continued in a wavelike pattern as time passed. Each time I felt this breeze, I would quickly begin to take in deep breaths. Deeper and deeper I found myself trying to fill my lungs with this aromatic peace. I could not seem to breathe in enough of that refreshment. For a short time, I was the only one to experience this, but soon after, my sister felt and smelled the same phenomena. The excitement for what was happening far exceeded the pain and fear that would come with our loss. Eventually, just as mysteriously as it had begun, the breeze and breathtaking aroma of roses ceased.

We continued to remain at Mom's bedside, not knowing what to expect, nor wanting to miss any detail. The emotional calm that came with the aromatic breeze remained in my heart as the evening gradually returned to its uneventful previous state. Slowly, the time ticked into the early morning hours of July 18. Light conversation occasionally filled the room, even in those quite early hours. We understood that every personal life journey is unique, yet even with trained professionals, no one could truly script the progression mom's journey would take. It was in those early morning hours that a family friend made the suggestion to me that perhaps my mom wouldn't want us at her bedside as she took her final breaths. I appreciated her words, however, I was not able to pull myself away from sitting at mom's bedside.

As I look back now, I believe this friend had revealed truth to me, yet at her side I remained. I recall glancing at the clock that was across the room, it was now 5:12 a.m. My siblings and I had been awake all night loving on our mom and taking in every moment we could while we still had her with us. Then, I felt a hand on my shoulder and was awakened by the words, "it is time". I had not realized I had fallen asleep in such a short instant. My first sight, when I opened my eyes was the clock, which now read 5:15 a.m. Then I looked at my mom. Mom's goal was to watch each of her children walk across the stage as they graduated high school, but instead, gathered at her bedside, together, my siblings and I walked her through an extremely peaceful exit from this world. I spent a few more moments with Mom. Her journey here on earth was over, however, her influence in my life was just beginning. I walked away knowing that I had been left with an unexplainable experience that would take spiritual ownership of the rest of my life.

As the deer pants for
streams of water, so my soul
pants for you, O God.
—Psalm 42:1

Chapter 4

F ollowing the death of my parents, now a young adult and
on my own, I searched earnestly for truth and guidance. You
see, not only did I no longer have parents, I also did not have
aunts or uncles, grandparents, or even close friends. At this time in
my life, I began searching for answers. I was living my life, but I
felt alone, abandoned, and orphaned. I wanted more, but what did
that mean?

There were a few things that kept me going. First, I knew that I
had no physical person in my life to lean on. This made my drive to
work hard and make good choices firm. I also knew that my parents'
belief in the church was immense. Because of this, my heart wanted
to honor my parents, but the path to do that was wide and confusing.
I was left alone to figure out what life was all about, and I was certain
that I did not want to mess it up. I felt as though I only had one
chance to get it right, and no one to lean on if I messed up. Finally,
I continued to experience the presence of God in my life in the same
unexplainable way I had at the time of Mom's passing. This did not
continue on a daily basis, but occasionally, there were times when
I would be alone, often when driving my car, that I would feel the
calm breeze and the aroma of fresh roses would fill the air. I will never
be able to explain this, but I know that when I have experienced it,
the same desire comes over me. I feel peace, and I begin to breathe in
deeply. It is so refreshing and calming. Over the years, as I have continued to experience this at random times, I have put an image to the

scent. I did not do this on that first night, but as this phenomenon continued, as I take in the beautiful smell, I have begun to picture an endless field of bright yellow roses blowing in the breeze. I am always taken back to the night my mom was taken from her earthly battle. These memories and experiences pushed me to search on.

I continued to attend Catholic masses. I also attended Lutheran services. Both spoke of God, both encouraged me to be involved in the church; both were filled with caring people trying to teach me why their faith was the right one. In all the subtle religious differences, I did find one thing in common; the Bible. I recognized that the Bible was the one book that had been there through the trials of the illnesses that my parents suffered. This book was in each church bench of either faith denomination that I chose to attend, and it had been available in my home. My desire for God's Word was there, yet I was unsure of what to do with it.

As a young child of reading age, I have memories of pulling a copy of our family's Children's Living Picture Bible off the bookshelf. I always had a strong desire to read it that began prior to my parent's health struggles. On more than one occasion, I remember taking that Bible off the shelf with the determination to read the whole book. I always started reading from the beginning—the genealogy of Jesus. It started with names; generations of names, and after many incorrectly articulated names, I would end at the birth of Jesus. That was enough! So many times I can recall desiring to get into that book. I would always start at the beginning, and I would always end after becoming exhausted and overwhelmed at the list of names.

I knew that the Bible was a key to my faith. It was talked about in both religions I had been researching. It was in my father's original Methodist faith. For a book that was so popular, I have to admit that I never once was encouraged to read it by a priest, family member, or a friend from the Catholic Church. Personally, however, I longed to read it—I believe this was planted in my heart naturally. I believe this was God showing up in my life in one of those times when I simply had not realized it.

As most young adults do, I spent time trying to figure out what direction I was supposed to go with my life. This included career paths, a desire for family, social needs, and spiritual direction. In each of those daunting searches, I found that I never neglected to seek biblical truth. I was always cautious of certain religions, and I knew that I would not allow myself to entertain the twisted beliefs of some religions. Although I pursued many paths, I continued to search for the truth in my faith.

I was confident that God was God. He was omnipotent and omniscient. I simply would not invest my time in any religion that believed in anything but this truth. My confusion arose when I saw so many different churches using the Bible yet telling me that there were different things that were true. In these churches, I noticed that as the listener, I was always being told the truths but never being encouraged to be the seeker. I found myself seeking a church that encouraged me to read my Bible—what a concept! I found this encouragement in the Christian faith!

I began to read more than just the genealogy of Jesus, which after reading my own Bible, I learned is found at the beginning of the book of Matthew. In addition to physically reading my Bible on my own, I also began to attend women's Bible studies. These took me deeper into the meaning of what I was reading as well as providing support when I had questions. I was excited! I dove into scripture and my studies, and most importantly, I asked questions. I wanted to be sure that what I was diving into was a river that was going to lead me to an ocean full of life and not a stream that would later dry up.

I continued on in my searching. At one point, my involvement in the Christian Church not only included Sunday services, but I was also attending three different Bible study groups. These groups were made up of a diverse population: a singles group, a women's group, and a mixed group of singles as well as married couples, some with kids and some without. I wanted to absorb aspects from each group. I took so much from each meeting, but I found that the key was in one clearly identical message. The message was the person of Jesus Christ.

As a "registered" Catholic as well as a "registered" Lutheran, I can honestly say that I had never been invited into getting to know this person of Jesus. I kept reading my Bible in groups as well as on my own. The Bible was teaching me the same message as my friends taught in their groups. Jesus was the only Way. Jesus was the Truth, and I desired the truth. I wanted to do the right thing. I knew the Bible was the center of many of the religions I had looked into. Those religions taught messages from the Bible, but the key that I was missing was the understanding that I needed to personally get to know the person of Jesus Christ.

I pursued the truth. I listened, and I changed my prayer. I asked God over and over to show me what was right and to keep me on the right path. I asked God for confirmation that what I was being told was true. I realized that there are good speakers in this world and anyone could talk you into believing their story, but I was only interested in knowing the true story. So I kept searching. I needed to know this person of Jesus Christ, but how exactly do I do that?

In my quiet time at home, I continued to read my Bible. That led to more questions. I would then take those questions to one of my three small groups, and I would boldly ask people to give me their thoughts. I would ask the same questions to different groups just to compare their answers. Then I would return home, and I would compare what they said with scriptures. My eyes were open to see more truth. The people I had chosen to surround myself with were different. They were joyful. They loved me unconditionally. They were excited to simply hang out together, have snacks or a meal, and "do life" together. I realized this was a family unit, which was a request I had so long ago prayed for God to return to me. The identity I had been living in this world was exhausting. I was alone, I had been abandoned, and I was an orphan. I had memories of my family, and I longed to have that once again; however, I didn't want someone there just to fill a void in my life. I began to recognize that

God was fulfilling my desire for family through the friends I had made in these groups.

My past experiences clearly proved that people leave you. I could categorize those losses into hurt relationships or circumstances; I had experienced both. My parents suffered physical disease, which brought pain and death. The imperfections of this world caused heartache, which brought a loss in many friendships over hurtful or unspoken words. Either way, the number of people who remained in my life, those people I could actually count on, was minimal. Through many years of being alone and experiencing pain, my rule of thumb for life was to push people away before they can leave or hurt you. I had lived a life trying to protect myself from the agony of relational hurts. I had learned how to live on the outside, yet be completely protected and locked up on the inside. I managed to make friends, but I kept them distant. I lived safe, and I was proud of that. I had done this for many years, but I was also on this journey where I was seeking truth.

I now found myself surrounded by people who loved life; people willing to share both joyful and painful life experiences together. This was not just one person or group. I had lived through this example in multiple sources. As an inquirer, I had thoroughly investigated those people and compared my data. In summary, what I found without any falter was that each of these people modeled to me a pathway that pointed in only one direction. That direction was toward a personal relationship with Jesus. I realized that I wanted what they had, but I was still confused. I kept praying and asking God for clarity. I still had many questions, and most importantly, I wanted to get it right. In my continued quest for answers, I never gave up meeting with friends. I found myself joining new groups, and I asked new questions, always hoping that I would finally get it right.

Outside of the groups, I tried to be in the church building as much as possible as well. Another area that drew me toward the Christian Church was through music. My love for music began with piano lessons in my early elementary years, and I was now finding that the Christian Church knew how to bring worship to life. Sunday services at the Christian Church were filled with live bands and heartfelt worship sessions. When I first began attending, I found this strange and a little awkward. This was contradictory to the hymnals that I grew up with in the Catholic Church; Christian worship was different. In the Christian service, there was not an organ on the altar—actually there wasn't even an altar. The Christian Church had a stage, and it was filled with vocalists, drummers, keyboard players, and guitarists. This worship was alive, and that seemed appropriate because what I had been reading about Jesus stated that he too was alive.

It didn't take too many weeks for me to be drawn to this new style of worship. I was able to follow along as the words were printed on large screens, and the rhythm was always pleasing to my ear. There were times when the songs were slower, with opportunity for self-reflection, but also times when the rhythm and words called for a celebration. No matter the style, worship was always followed by true biblical teaching where the congregation was encouraged to actually pull out their Bibles and read along. All of these details fed into my heart little trickles of confirmation that I was on the right path, yet I continued to search.

The Christian Church that I had been attending often hosted what they called "night of worship," and due to my love of music, I attended as many as I could. This was a time to get together with the church body, and rather than have a full sermon, we would enjoy an extended period of live worship. Those in attendance were welcome to move around, sing, or pray together. I looked forward to these times of worship. I was single (twenty-one years old) and desperately looking for confirmation and direction. I felt as though I was beginning to receive that, and on one particular night of worship, it came louder and more unexpected than I could ever have dreamed.

March 6, 1996, was a day that would change my life forever. Once again, I had decided to attend the planned night of worship service. I had made many friends at that point, and I looked forward to the worship. As the service began, I quickly took my seat in the third or fourth row center of the church. As the worship began, I knew I was in the right place. I had not become comfortable with raising my hands in worship, but people around me felt free to do so. I later learned that this too is a biblical practice. As I looked around that night, I saw so many faces of those who had come along side of me. These were people who had seen my heart and understood my desire to search for the truth. They were excited to see me growing in my faith. I was truly beginning to realize that I was surrounded not only by friends, but these people had become family. I took advantage of the night and worshipped through the music with all my heart.

While celebrating the journey I had been taken on and recognizing the family God had blessed me with, my worship was interrupted. Above all the guitars, drums, and voices of the people, I heard a voice, loud and clear, call out to me stating, "It's time to walk alone." It was such a strong voice, and so obvious. There was no doubt as to the clarity of the words I heard, but I did question who had spoken these words. I looked to my right and saw the faces of some of the people who had held my hand along the way. These were the faces of people who prayed for me and were modeling their faith by attending the night of worship. In that moment, I knew that I had clearly heard a male voice above all the worship, and I looked around in confusion. It appeared as though no one else had heard this distinct interruption. As I looked around, I could see that everyone else continued, uninterruptedly, singing praises and enjoying the night. I quickly recognized that I was being called out. "It's time to walk alone" replayed in my head, and I immediately realized what it meant.

God had been faithful to answer every one of my questions. He provided friends and family to support and love me on my journey. He knew my heart and even my doubt, and he gave me the time I needed to gather all of my research. Through my searching, he was faithful to show up in my relationships, yet again, I was completely unaware. In this moment, it was different. In this moment, he was revealing himself to me in a real and obvious way. I had prayed for clarity and direction, and he answered by speaking directly to me. In that moment, during that night of worship, I heard his voice gently but firmly calling out to me, "It's time to walk alone." I knew that I was being called to step out and let go of the physical relationships I had developed. I was not being asked to leave those people, but to take my faith to a more intimate level with Jesus. I was being asked to walk alone …

I had spent so much time living in fear of being hurt and believing that it was my job to push people away before they could hurt me. In my mind, I had decided that living alone was the only way to protect myself. For many years this was the safe place to live, and I was successful at it. However, along my spiritual journey, I learned this personal belief was actually a lie and it was hurting me from the inside. God had given me the time I needed to relearn that people were trustworthy. I was beginning to recognize that I had true friends and family in these relationships and just as I was beginning to experience these wonderful things, I was being told, "It's time to walk alone."

The path of walking alone was the way I had summarized many years of my childhood. My new relationships were nurturing joy within me and rebuilding my trust. I didn't want to be alone anymore, and I had been filling that void with my many choices of involvement. On that night, my joy and excitement for worship was quickly replaced with confusion. I didn't understand where the voice had come from, and I certainly did not want to choose to be alone. After just a short time of contemplation, I made a quick decision. I chose to run.

I grabbed all the material things I had brought with me that night, and I took off toward the main entrance of the building. As I ran toward the door, I replayed the words I had heard over in my head. During my rapid exit toward the door, I continued to process what was happening. Thankfully, I realized the importance of what was occurring. I saw that this was a life-changing moment. I recognized that I could walk out the door, which would allow me to return to the life that I had built. I would be happy, and most importantly, I would be safe emotionally and relationally. The other option was to turn around and accept the gift that was before me. I knew that being alone was terrifying, but in that moment, I was not feeling terrified. I chose to turn around and head back into the worship center. Tears were rushing down my cheeks as I was embraced by people I did not even know. I simply verbally admitted "I want Jesus," and the physical response was unexpected. I was swarmed by more people who gathered around me and prayed for me right then and there. No questions asked. I prayed that night, and I asked Jesus into my heart to be my personal Savior. I answered the call and chose that night to walk alone, yet to my surprise, I was far from alone! I was surrounded by people whom I had never met as well as those who had been walking with me. We prayed and cried and celebrated my choice to follow Jesus. In my search, God had blessed me day after day with more friends and more family than any person could ever have dreamed of, and most importantly, God had been faithful to be there for me every step of the way. I accepted his call to walk alone, and that allowed me to take my faith deeper on a personal level. Following that night, I continued to participate in Bible studies and serve in various activities. As I was called that night to walk alone, I have found that I have never had to truly walk alone on this journey.

So we fix our eyes not on what
is seen, but on what is unseen.
For what is seen is temporary,
but what is unseen is eternal.
—2 Corinthians 4:18

Chapter 5

I didn't write my story. If I had that opportunity, I probably would have deleted all the chapters that covered my early years up until the point that I accepted Christ on March 6, 1996. But as I have walked with the Lord, and chosen to be thankful for the story that he wrote, I was led to this verse in 2 Corinthians: "So we fix our eyes not on what is seen, but on what is unseen. For what is seen is temporary, but what is unseen is eternal." I wish I had written the date in my Bible of exactly when God had revealed this verse to me, but the date doesn't matter. More importantly, I have held fast to it as my life verse ever since, and I have tried to focus more on the end of the passage—"what is seen is temporary, but what is unseen is eternal."

God is in control. He was in control through all of the cancer battles my family faced and the remissions we dealt with time and time again. He was in control when I was a teenager acting so far out of control while grieving the loss of my dad. He was in control as I walked alongside my mother's casket, still a teenager, not knowing where life would take me. Abandoned, orphaned, and alone—God was in control. And now as a young adult, God gently reminded me of this through his words, "fix our eyes not on what is seen, but on what is unseen." I did not know the impact that verse would have in my life until I began the fall of 2004.

In the years following my mother's death, I continued on with my faith journey. In early fall of 2004, my efforts transitioned from seeking deeper spiritual answers to a satisfying clarity. I knew that God was again working wonderful plans into my life. I had been walking with the Lord for almost ten years at that point and had faithfully dedicated my heart to learning His truths, His Word, and His plan for my life. At times, this was difficult for me. I was far from a perfect person, and I remain as such. Many times during my walk, I found that I had to have trust in people. As a result of my childhood, this was terrifying for me. In many situations, I found myself doubting if I was making the right choice to trust. I would remind myself how bad it felt to be hurt and how easy it was to push people away to remain safe. But I knew that God's Word was faithful, and as long as I had Him as my center and I tried to live my life according to His ways, I would be safe. This clarity allowed me to move forward.

As I had continued in my efforts to develop my commitment to my faith in Christ, I had added attendance to women's retreats as part of my faith walk. This was a great way to get away from the demands of life and reflect on God and His plans for me. I often would gather a group of girlfriends and plan on attending different women's conferences together. I learned of a retreat in the fall of 2004, and I was eager to attend. I began to ask friends if they would join me, but none whom I asked were available. Without hesitation, I decided to attend the retreat alone. I felt peaceful about my decision and was looking forward to my time away. Excited, I signed up alone, drove there alone, and once there, found a corner bunk alone where I began to unpack my overnight belongings. Reflecting on my walk, I knew that God had asked me to "walk alone." Moving forward in his calling, I knew I would be all right on this particular weekend.

It was not surprising, when I arrived at the retreat, that I recognized many familiar faces. I had been involved in multiple groups while seeking answers, and I had become acquaintances with many people over the years. Although I did not know these women closely, it was refreshing to reconnect with friends from my past. As do most retreats, the opening night included welcome games, icebreakers, and worship, all of which helped to rekindle memories as well as make new friends. On paper it was everything that I had hoped for, but spiritually, it was exactly what God had prepared.

At this time, I was actively aware of God in my life, but completely unaware and unprepared for the plan that he was about to reveal to me. Opening activities and icebreakers were followed with worship, and I again found myself in a room full of people whose hearts were on fire for drawing closer to God. My love for music allowed me to truly enjoy the experience, and it was an amazing time to be in God's presence. I was joyfully soaking it all in.

The next morning, by choice, I eagerly began alone. I had come prepared with a preplanned routine. I planned to be up and showered before the others. I am not sure why this is my pattern—as my husband can tell you, I am the last one to get up at home. But being away and outside my comfort zone, I had planned on having my morning exactly as I had envisioned. After my shower, I had planned on finding a secluded place outdoors to have my morning quiet time. At home, I did not have fields of wooded bliss to walk in or sit and enjoy. I was looking forward to finding a quaint little area where I could hear the animals scurrying about and I would be isolated from others and free to read and pray as I wished.

I love to pray, and even more, I love to pray out loud. Jesus is my best friend, and I talk with him just as I talk to any other friend. I figured finding a solitary place was the best way to do this rather than in a room being shared with fifteen other women. I found a picnic table stashed away in the wooded fields. I watched my time because I did not want to miss the morning worship or the teaching that was planned to start the day off. My time alone was refreshing. Occasionally, I was joined by a curious squirrel while the crisp morning air surrounded me. Traditionally, I do not enjoy the cool air, but this was the perfect setting for allowing me to be still and draw near to God. I finished up my quiet time and hurried to the chapel to begin what I thought would be an easy and enjoyable morning of spiritual growth.

Again, the worship drew me in. I fell mesmerized by the faith-fulness of God. He was alive in the room, and everyone was celebrat-ing their personal walks with him. During that worship God began a stirring in my heart, which he continued through the words the keynote speaker delivered in the morning session. I was unprepared.

After years of spiritual searching and what I thought was open-ing my heart, I was completely unaware that I had so much pain that remained locked inside me. I had no idea that my past was keeping me from the plans that he had for me. But God is in control. He knows me, and he knows my needs. It was in that morning session that God began to peel away the deeper layers in my heart.

I felt the worship moving in my soul. In an unfamiliar way, I began to feel my heart race. I could tell that emotions were well-ing up inside of me, and I was not in agreement with that. In my adult life, I continued to hide my emotion and was persistent in my endeavor to ban tears from my life. Although I felt I had grown quite a bit as far as relationships were concerned, I still refused to relive the emotional torment from the early years of my life. I learned to survive through the busyness of extracurricular activities and through successfully eliminating the emotion that came with the memories. But on that retreat, I did not have any activities to distract me.

In that morning session, my emotions became real. This was new territory for me as I sat there confused and afraid. How would I handle this situation? My heart continued to race, and I felt my respi-rations increase. I was repeatedly taking deep breaths to try and calm the storm of emotion that was welling up inside me. My eyes were burning from fighting back the tears. I had a beverage next to me, and I repeatedly took swigs from the soda can, swallowing as hard as I could, hoping the fizz and bubbles would clear the lump in my throat. I looked around and took a census of all the people surround-ing me. I knew that I could lean on any friend in this room, which was the opposite of where I had come from. As I had matured in my faith, I knew in this situation that I could find support. I knew that I didn't have to be alone in this, but I was completely overwhelmed. I had no idea where this emotion was coming from, I simply could not explain what was happening. As I had done in the past, I again chose to run. I found myself, for the second time, running toward the door of the chapel, so eager to get away. I didn't know what was going on, but I was not going to stick around to experience it. Unlike the first time I chose to run, this time, I did not stop. My body was physically overwhelmed and ready to break, and this terrified me. I had to get away, and I did not hesitate to hustle out the chapel door and toward the open field as quickly as I could.

Breathing heavily and with tears pouring down my cheeks, I understood that I was hurting, but I was confused as to why. I had had such a good evening with friends and a sweet morning reading my Bible and praying. The emotions came in such strong waves that I could not hold any tears back, and I had no choice but to stand in the field and sob. I thought I was alone, but then I felt a hand gently grab my shoulder, causing me to turn. When I had, I found that I had been joined by a dear friend who had been in the chapel with me and observed my quick departure. In that moment, she encouraged me to talk with her. She wanted me to share with her what was going on. She truly wanted to support me in any way that she could. The problem was, I really had no idea what I was experiencing. I could not share what I did not know. I tried to explain to her that my tears were heavy but unexplainable, but I am sure she didn't believe me. It felt nice to have someone there to support me. I wish I could have offered her more, but I simply did not know why I was so emotional. Her support and comfort allowed me to get ahold of myself and dry up my tears. Together we returned to the group, where we participated in the remaining planned activities. Needless to say, I finished the retreat exhausted and confused with my experience.

One week after the retreat, I found myself in church again, enjoying the Sunday service with my family. On that particular day, we had decided to go out for lunch after service. I had spent the week reflecting on what had happened at the retreat and debating what my emotional surge was all about. In my walk with the Lord,

I had learned that confusion was not part of his plan, and as that Sunday approached, my confusion was transforming into clarity. As I reflected that week on what may have caused such an extreme emotional surge, I grew more confident that I was not the emotional basket case that everyone had witnessed on the outside. I was becoming more convinced that God was planning something big, and he just wanted to make sure he had my attention.

For where two or three
come together in my name,
there am I with them.
—Matthew 18:20

Chapter **6**

A t the time, we had two boys: a nine-year-old and a two-year-old. They enjoyed eating out at restaurants, and we did as well. On this particular Sunday, just a week after the retreat, our family decided to enjoy a quick meal at a local diner before heading home for the day. We chose one that we had not been to as a family but my husband had enjoyed multiple times with his work travels. The boys were excited as this eatery offered quite a few choices of ice creams and dessert treats to complement their meals. We took our time in making a decision from the menu, and then we chose our seats. While we were waiting for our order to arrive at the table, I felt that I could not hold my excitement in any longer. I strategically sent the boys away from the table for a drink refill, napkins, and condiments, so that I could have a quick private moment with my husband. I was feeling more certain about what had caused my emotional surge at the retreat, and I couldn't wait to reveal to him what I felt was becoming so clear to me. In the short moment that we were alone, I looked at him and excitedly said, "I think we are pregnant!"

My husband is a natural in the world of fatherhood. He loves children, and we often joke that he remains to be one himself. The news of an additional little one to climb on his lap and play pranks on Mom was immediately welcomed. As the boys returned to our table, our food arrived as well. Needless to say, we devoured our lunch quickly and immediately followed the meal by a trip to the local drugstore. The drive home seemed to take forever, followed by an eternity of waiting on the pregnancy test results, which in reality was only three minutes. All of our waiting paid off when the test confirmed that we were being blessed with a third child. I knew without any doubt what God had been doing at the retreat. Just as he first did many years earlier at my church's night of worship, God was getting my attention in a mighty and powerful way. He knew me better than I knew myself, and it was obvious that in order to get my attention, He would have to take drastic measures. Fortunately, as I continued to grow in my spiritual life, I was beginning to recognize his voice. I felt confident that I knew how the next chapter in our lives would read: more joy and laughter in our home as we would prepare for this little addition. However, my thoughts could not have been further from the truth. Although I had drawn various exciting conclusions from our news, I was completely unaware of the twist that was to come in the story that God had actually written for me.

Following the confirmation on the home pregnancy test, I scheduled an appointment with my physician for medical confirmation. I knew this would include routine blood tests and a dreaded weight check, but most exciting of all was knowing that we would hear confirmation of the probable due date for our little one. Not only was I was excited about the scheduled appointment, but my husband was as well. In the past, he had always attended doctor visits that had to do with our babies, and I knew that this pregnancy would be no different. In addition, we have always been a family that leans more on the traditional side, so we knew that we would do our best to move through the pregnancy without using advanced medical interventions, if possible. Our decision allowed the gender of our baby to remain a surprise as well as decline medications for delivery assistance. I had come to a place in my heart where these things were of little value to me. My faith was stronger than it had ever been, and I knew that God already knew the gender of our child. I also knew that I could lean on him through the pain of the delivery, and I wanted to trust in him in both of these ways rather than on medical interventions. I am not opposed to medications and medical interventions by any means. I am a nurse by profession and intervene with these methods on a regular basis. My decision was solely based on the fact that I had grown spiritually, and I knew that God had never left me or expected me to walk through life alone. I was willing to trust in him, even if it meant a natural childbirth and not having gender-specific items at the time of the baby's arrival. It was going to be all right either way, and we had chosen to let God surprise us and guide us. The first visit with our doctor went as expected. My blood work, vital signs, and other labs were collected, and most importantly, we were confirmed to be expecting and given an expected arrival date for early July 2005. We were ecstatic and knew the next step would be the adventure of telling family and friends.

That moment would present itself just a few days later, as we had planned to attend a family birthday celebration. Knowing that this would be a large gathering of aunts, uncles, grandparents, and cousins, we felt it was the perfect place to share our news all at once. We are not very creative people, but we did want to come up with a somewhat different way to make our announcement. We threw around multiple ideas, but found both our lack of creativity as well as time prevented us from preparing an extraordinary revelation. We decided to simply place our big announcement in handwritten form in the birthday card. We simply signed the card "Happy Birthday, Love"—and then wrote each of our names in family order. We ended with the addition of another line that simply said "and Baby."

The day of the party had finally arrived, which was not a moment too soon. We could hardly keep our secret in any longer. Family members greeted one another and laughter began to fill the room. A birthday meal was shared and we knew that gift time was inevitably approaching. As the family gathered around the table to share in the opening of gifts, we waited patiently as we watched our card draw closer and closer to the top of the pile. We expected an immediate response; however, in alignment with our lack of creativity, the plan fell through. As the card took a few passes around to family members, our excitement changed to humor. We realized that people really do not read cards and our news was being tossed around carelessly among the family. After multiple card passes, my husband broke the cycle by asking "Who is that card from?" indicating our card. A quick response was given based off the first name on the card. The party guests still had not heard the news. He asked again, being more specific this time, "Who is the card from?" And then he added, "Read all of the names," placing emphasis on his additional comment. Realizing now that there was a secret message in the card, people started grabbing for it quickly. Finally, one person got a firm hold of it, and the names were read aloud. Shouts of elation filled the room as the additional "baby" signature was read aloud. The response was exactly what we had hoped for. This baby was already deeply loved, and the news of its arrival filled everyone's hearts with joy.

The party was just the start of many more opportunities to share our news as we encountered different friends and family members each week. The response from everyone was pure joy and excitement for our newest addition. Eventually, the excitement calmed, and our days returned to routine schedules, which included homeschooling and caring for various additional children in my home. Our house was always busy and full of love. I feel that this was a direct result of the abundant blessings I had received through many wonderful friends and mentors. Over the years, these ladies had modeled for me what I also desired in my home. I had learned to listen closely to my mentors on many levels, including as a mother, teacher, and as a Christian.

In December of that year, one of my mentors and fellow homeschool mom reached out to me and simply asked if she could pray for me. I have learned over the years that there is always room for prayer in my life, so I was not going to turn her offer down. We tried multiple times to schedule a meeting but were met with repetitive conflict in our schedules due to busy family obligations. She did not give up on trying to meet, and her persistence finally paid off. I then waited patiently for that date to arrive.

Recalling that I grew up in a household where faith and prayer were not conjoined, this was one of those areas I had long searched for answers many years back. In those years of searching for what true prayer was to look like, I again turned to my one and only faithful source, the Bible, and again I was not let down. In the Bible, I found many examples of prayer, and I personally concluded how important prayer was. Learning to pray was not something that I just picked up on from reading the examples in the Bible. As I had done repeatedly along my faith journey, I again asked questions about the area of prayer. I sought out role models for clarification and direction, and I compared what I had heard, seen, and read. I was blessed with prayer mentors who invited me to walk alongside them and join them as they took time away to pray. I asked God for wisdom as I opened my heart and learned how to pray.

I learned that prayer did not always involve a speaking role. As a former Catholic, I had learned many scripted prayers as a child and was asked to recite them as proof of my work. Today, as a believer in prayer, I would not argue against those prayers. I would not hesitate to recite an Our Father, because I know this prayer was taken directly from the Bible, quoting Jesus as he called out to his Father. I knew this was provided as an example of how I should pray as well. Furthermore, I learned that prayer was so much more than just reciting those memorized words. Prayer is listening. Prayer is quieting your heart, putting aside your beliefs, setting down your worries and your plans and saying, "God, I am here to listen." I found that this was not easy to do. I would have to say that prayer was uncomfortable at first. I questioned if I knew how to listen and if I would have the correct words to say. I trusted my mentors, and I pushed through. Now, as an adult, I understand the power of prayer. I would not want to live my life without it. Today I welcome prayer in many forms, whether I am praying for someone, quietly praying alone, or receiving prayer from a friend. I get lost in the quiet peace it brings. Prayer is not work or a duty as a Christian. Prayer is a gift that allows me to sit in God's presence, to learn, and to grow in my faith. As my friend and I planned to meet together for prayer, I was excited to hear what God would share with us.

When the time came for us to meet, I remember being filled with such excitement. My friend was eager to pray. She did not know exactly what she was praying for, but she knew God had placed it on her heart to pray for me. Fortunately, I was willing to sit and listen. I cannot tell you the exact words she spoke that afternoon, but I can tell you that my heart and mind were completely drawn into listening. My heart was calmed to an unimaginable level, and I was at complete and total peace. As her words poured out around me, I felt as though everything else was pushing itself further away. I was being drawn nearer and nearer to God. I didn't hear His voice, but I knew He was there. As I heard the tranquil tones of her voice fade away, I knew that God was calling me to his attention. I knew that God had spoken excitement into my friend's heart, and I knew the message that she was sharing was a nudge for me to realize that God was about to do something very big in my life. I did not leave that time of prayer with specific clarification as to what God was preparing for me, but I did walk away with my eyes wide open, ready to see what God was planning next.

It is not for you to know the
times or dates the Father has
set by his own authority. But
you will receive power when
the Holy Spirit comes on you.
—Acts 1:7–8

Chapter 7

The excitement for our baby extended far into the hearts of
our family and did not waver as the holidays approached.
One of the first Christmas gifts we opened that year was
a "Baby's First Christmas" ornament from a family member. We
laughed and giggled as we talked about what next year's Christmas
would be like with a new baby joining the family. Opening gifts for
our baby made the arrival seem sooner than it truly was and brought
joy to our hearts as we continued to celebrate Christmas with family.

Following the holidays, we resumed life as usual. I was at home
most days with the kids, and the busyness of life kept us going. I was
able to keep things moving successfully, not because of my super-
powers as a mom, but as a result of another skill I had learned while
on my journey for answers. In addition to reading my Bible, praying, and having strong friends for accountability, I had also learned
the importance of taking a verse from scripture, reflecting on it, and
memorizing it. As I had found with learning to pray, this too was
a challenge at first. I am not the best at memorization, but once I
accepted the challenge and put my heart into it, I was able to accom-
plish this, and I developed a love for memorizing scripture.

One of the first scriptures I had memorized was Philippians
4:11–12: "For I have learned to be content whatever the circumstances. I know what it is to be in need, and I know what it is to have
plenty. I have learned the secret of being content in any and every
situation, whether well fed or hungry, whether living in plenty or in

want." I grew up in a loving Catholic family that was later ripped apart from the devastation that cancer brings. I taught myself how to protect my heart and how to get through life by pushing people away. My past had been a shameful burden full of heartache; however, as an adult, I had now learned to be content, which only came from the peace of my daily quiet time. In those moments each day, I would strive to find a place to be alone with my best friend, Jesus. In these times, I could separate from the challenges and commitments of daily life and seek his will and plans for me. In these times, I would find myself doing a "heart check" and asking if I was living the way scriptures called me to live. This was a time to be refreshed and encouraged. Considering that my life was very busy, I did not want to miss these daily opportunities to refuel.

In my search for building a strong faith walk, I adopted the practice of starting each day with my quiet time. This would be a time to read from my Bible, reflect on my lifestyle, pray for guidance and wisdom and listen for direction and encouragement. Certainly, there are days that life jumps ahead of me where my quiet time would be delayed or postponed; however, I make a gallant effort to start every morning in quiet reflection. I look forward to learning something new in scripture, I desire the peace I feel when sitting in *his* presence, and I long for the reset each new day can bring. This had become my daily practice, and Saturday, January 15, 2005, was no different.

The kids were playing downstairs with a friend who had spent the night. Knowing they were safe and content with their activities, I took full advantage of the quietness in my kitchen. I pulled out my Bible to begin my daily devotions. Typically, I choose a book of the Bible and read one chapter in that book each day until the book has been completed, and then I move on, choosing a new book from the Bible to read; not necessarily in chronological order. I have found that reading books of the Bible one at a time was more comprehensible than my previous tactic as a child of trying to read the entire Bible in one setting.

I typically pray before I begin reading and invite the Holy Spirit to be a part of my quiet time. I ask for the Holy Spirit to prepare me for what I am about to read, to teach me, and to show me how I can be a better Christian through what I was learning. That particular morning, I was preparing to begin the book of Acts. I was eager to get started in a new book and I was open to learning more about the early church. Since the boys were downstairs playing, I was able to find a comfortable place in my kitchen to have my quiet time. (Sometimes, I would hide on the staircase or find another creative place just to keep kids from climbing on me for five minutes.) As routine played out, I opened my quiet time in prayer that may have included asking for prayer for family members or situations I may have been facing at that time, but most importantly, I would ask to hear the message God wanted to teach me for that day. On that particular morning, I also specifically prayed for our baby.

My husband and I had been looking through various baby name books, and we were having a difficult time choosing the perfect name for our little one. Not knowing if our baby was a boy or a girl also made it more complicated, but we had agreed to settle on two names for each gender. We were nowhere near having a single name in either direction. We had joked about many names and also felt confusion. We recognized what a huge responsibility it is to choose the name that this child will grow up with their entire life. Up to this point, our discussions had never ended with a conclusion, but just multiple possibilities and the expectation of future discussions to come. Having learned that I can pray about absolutely anything, I felt I should add this prayer for guidance and wisdom into my opening prayer for that day. I recall praying specifically something similar to, "Lord, you already know this child, and you already call it by name. Please give us wisdom to name this baby as you have already."

I then moved on with excitement to begin my journey in the book of Acts. The book opens with chapter 1 speaking about Jesus's return to his disciples after his suffering on the cross. It spoke about how he took forty days to appear to his followers and then how he gave instruction to wait. His instruction was to wait for a gift that they would receive and spoke about this being the gift of the Holy Spirit. I continued to read and arrived at verse 8, "but you will receive power when the Holy Spirit comes on you; and you will be my witnesses." Without a moment's hesitation, as I read through that scripture, the peaceful breeze that I had experienced many years earlier at my mother's bedside surrounded me once again. As the breeze surrounded me in my kitchen, the peace surrounding me also increased greatly. In the same instant of feeling this new level of calm, I heard an audible voice call out "Rose." I cannot explain this. Not only had I heard a voice calling out, but I felt the presence of complete and total peace. Immediately in that moment, I knew without any question that my child's name had just been spoken to me, and there was no question as to whose voice it was that had done the speaking. My first reaction to hearing the name was literally me, stating out loud, "I don't like that name." However; the spirit that filled the room pushed me further.

In that same moment of certainty, I did what I knew best to do; I grabbed my Bible even tighter and began eagerly searching the name Rose in scripture. My first thought was that there had to be someone in scripture named Rose that I had just not yet read about. I looked in every place possible to find the story of a godly woman named Rose; however, I did not find any such connection. My next action was to grab the baby name book that my husband and I had been using in our own search. I turned alphabetically to the *R* section and scrolled down to find the name Rose. I read out loud the meaning of the name. It simply stated "beautiful." As I read this meaning out loud, the peace that I had felt moments before surrounded me again like a gentle wind blowing across my kitchen. My eyes welled up with tears; but these tears were different.

In the past, tears symbolized sadness and heartbreak. I had decided that tears were a sign of weakness or being needy. I had taught myself how to turn off the faucet of emotion, and I had mastered the ability to hold any and all glimpses of deep emotion. I was the queen of dry tear ducts, and I had found a false sense of pride in that accomplishment.

For many years I found contentment in that until the night back in 1996 when I decided to allow Christ into my heart. That night, I was filled with tears, and I let them fall. I was safe, and I was celebrating the decision I had made. I knew my life was going to be different from that day forward, and I had been joined with so many people celebrating with me. Those tears were real, but they had not fully broken the chains of emotional withdrawal that I had locked up for so many years. In that moment, I was joyful, but God knew that I still had many layers to work through. I was now able to see that He had always remained faithful in breaking down my emotional walls. He began back when my mom had bestowed unconditional forgiveness on me, and many years later, he continued on the night that I invited Christ into my heart. He knew the layers were deep, and he slowly continued to peel away my walls. Next, God had shown up in a mighty way at the women's retreat. It was there that I was powerless to hold back my emotions. The struggle I experienced in that moment was confusing, but I knew during that experience I was safe as well. I did not know what God was doing, nor had I realized that God was only beginning to prepare me for something bigger. In that moment, after running, and with resistance, I allowed the tears to flow; but I was not able to explain to my friend what was causing my tears.

Now, on this winter January morning, sitting alone in my kitchen, the tears again flowed down my cheeks. These tears were not tears of pain, nor were they tears of failure, defeat, or confusion. These were tears of peace! I had no idea that tears could be a refreshing expression of excitement, joy, and hope. I sat in the moment, treasuring the feeling of absolute peace and contentment. I was in awe that God would choose to speak to me in such a profound and audible way, but I was grateful and full of excitement that he had. I let the tears flow, and during that episode of peace and growth, I began to laugh. I enjoyed my tears, and I knew that the verse I had read was true, "You will receive power when the Holy Spirit comes on you; and you will be my witnesses." I had done nothing extraordinary; I simply showed up. I was willing to listen and learn while God did the rest.

I grabbed my journal and quickly wrote every moment of that experience down, trying not to miss a single detail. I wrote with passion through this peaceful cry. I accepted the tears, knowing they were refreshing and confirming that my God can do impossible things; my job was to be open to his truth and let him lead. I summed up my journal entry that day with the words, "I believe God is giving us a beautiful Rose to love." I knew that from a medical standpoint, we would have to wait almost another six months to find out if I was crazy or not, but I was pretty sure that God wanted to get my attention in a big way, and he knew that revealing the gender of my baby through calling her by name would be a good attention-grabber. He had my attention! As I stated, I always begin and end my quiet time in prayer. On that day, I joyfully concluded my prayer time by asking God to "please move my husband's heart to also like that name."

About a week later, my husband and I planned a date night at a local coffee shop. Up to this point, I was unsure how to tell him about my experience, and I also felt that he was going to think I had totally lost my mind. We ordered our drinks and sat to enjoy a time of uninterrupted conversation. It didn't take long for me to begin, and I simply started with, "I have something to tell you." His inquisitive eyes looked at me with curiosity, and I began to share the story of what I had experienced in our kitchen just a few days prior. Most importantly, I shared with him how I faithfully asked God for guidance for our upcoming parental decision of naming our baby. I then went into detail about my experience in the kitchen and tried to explain the enormous amount of peace that I had felt. Finally, I boldly shared with my husband the punchline—"We are having a girl, and her name is Rose."

It felt amazing to have stepped out in faith and share the truth of this bizarre experience that had taken place. Who in this world would believe such a story? I had asked myself that countless times over the last week, but I knew what God had done, and I knew that my husband would trust and support me in this. I looked across the table at him, expectantly waiting for a response, and he simply smiled back. I knew that he had heard my heart and was in complete trust in the situation. Being a man of humor, he simply responded with, "Did God tell you her middle name?" The laughter that filled our table was refreshing. I knew he did not think I had lost my mind. Our conversation then transitioned to discussing middle names to go with Rose, in addition to debating some quality names for a little boy—just in case I had messed this whole "voice in my kitchen" thing up. I knew where my faith had taken me, and I knew what I believed. God can do whatever *he* wants, and he can choose to speak to whomever he wants, when and how he wants. But I also knew that I was human, and this experience was very different, probably even considered explainable or false to most people. The peace I had in that moment was undeniable, but my human comprehension left a small window of my mind open to doubt. On our date, we were able to finalize both our girl and our boy baby names. We left completely aware that God had grabbed our attention and we had our eyes wide open to see what plans he had for us next.

For my thoughts are not your
thoughts, neither are your ways
my ways, declares the Lord.
Isaiah 55:8

Chapter 8

The following weeks were what one would describe as normal. School for the kids, providing childcare for friends, housework, and sporting events filled the calendar. Life carried on as usual. Now having baby names chosen, we were able to begin thinking about other exciting plans for our newest addition. Just as eager as my husband was about choosing baby names, he was also passionate about wanting to share his ideas for nursery themes, choosing toys, and attending doctor visits. Nothing stopped him from enjoying our pregnancies. At times, he would have to arrange his work schedule around some of the appointments or drive over quickly on his lunch, but he would not think of missing a chance to see our baby on the screen. There were times I questioned his intentions as truthfully being based around the desire to see how much weight I had gained—but either way, he was always present. March 4, 2005, was no exception.

This was an exciting day for us as we were scheduled for our first ultrasound. We had already heard our baby's heartbeat in previous visits, but today we were looking forward to actually seeing our little one on the monitor. To see the tiny hands and feet that were kicking away inside my belly and maybe capture an image of what the baby's facial features would look like was electrifying. Many of our friends would get excited about ultrasounds appointments because this would be a time to reveal the gender of their little ones, but we had every intention of keeping this a secret, and this appointment would not change our plans. We had planned for the boys to spend the morning with a fellow homeschool family and dear friends. They were excited for a change in their morning routine as well as having some time with friends. We dropped off the boys and headed to the appointment.

Joking, holding hands, and giddy was how we approached the main entrance of the hospital. We sat patiently in the office area with joy in our hearts until we were called back by the technician. In the room, the visit began with traditional questions and an easy exchange of smiles and laughter as we talked back and forth with our ultrasound technician. The technician turned the monitor on, and immediately we could see the black-and-white fuzzy screen that would soon reveal our baby's image. After applying the warm gel to my abdomen, the technician began to slide the ultrasound wand back and forth through the gel. My husband and I joked with eager anticipation. We heard various clicks as the technician tapped on the computer keyboard and drafted various markings to support the information she was gathering. We continued to wait patiently as she organized her data, noticing that the monitor image we were looking at seemed difficult to decipher. I had seen many ultrasound photos in the past. Although they were never of professional quality, I knew they provided a gentle image of a growing baby, yet this was not what we were in view of just yet. We waited in eager expectation for the image to clear up. We were ready to get the first glimpse of our baby. We waited longer. We could hear the tiny heartbeat and felt growing excitement, but the technician seemed to be taking her time making attempts to clear up the monitor to allow us any quality view.

Eventually, our laughter and playful comments grew to concern as we realized the technician was not going to correct the monitor. Her words "We have a problem" broke the silence, and my witty husband then chimed in with, "What? Is it twins?" The technician did not make any verbal response to his attempt at humor. She continued to tap on her keyboard and completed gathering detailed images. Finally, she reconnected with us and shared her concerns regarding an extremely low level of amniotic fluid surrounding the baby. She explained to us that the low level of fluid was the reason behind the distorted image. She explained that the amniotic fluid acts as a type of image enhancer, and our baby did not have any fluid around it; thus she could not capture a quality photo. Her words and explanation didn't sound too serious to us; however, her tone of voice and concerned expression communicated so much more. She excused herself from the room, and shortly after her departure, we were escorted into a regular exam room to wait on our physician.

Only a short time had passed before the door opened, and the longtime friendly face of my physician entered the room. I had seen him many times over the years and am grateful to say that he had delivered each of the boys, ten and three years ago. I had learned over the years, with previous (although slight) complications, to trust in his medical expertise. In addition to his medical expertise, I had also come to respect him as a person. Not only had he gotten to know me as a patient; he also had taken the time to build a relationship with my husband as well. Over the years of being under his care, it was obvious that he took his oath as a physician seriously, as well as also possessing a genuine love for people.

The doctor sat down with us and with a deep and heavy breath, he proceeded to inform us that our baby had a rare condition called bilateral renal agenesis. I knew the term *renal* had to do with the kidneys, but I was unsure what the complete diagnosis meant. Our physician then went on to tell us that our baby had not developed kidneys during the early stages of growth. We were then informed that around the eleventh week of pregnancy, this should have occurred. Considering how tiny a baby is at eleven weeks, and the organs are even smaller, physicians typically wait until closer to the twenty-week mark to perform initial ultrasounds (unless there are special situations) for development and care evaluations. Twenty weeks was approximately the timing in weeks that we were on this particular day.

The physician's voice broke as he gently provided education regarding our baby's condition. He offered to address all of our concerns; however, in those moments we could not compile anything too deep to formulate good questions. He continued to share with us other complications the baby would have, most dramatic would be underdeveloped lungs and the inability to complete gas exchange necessary for breathing. He then began to gently inform us of the limited hope of any chance of our baby surviving. He stated that in his time of practice, he had seen this condition only one other time, and that child did not make it. Although the news was grim, he was able to reassure us that in that moment, both myself and our baby were perfectly safe. My body was providing all of the nourishment and oxygen our baby needed to thrive in my womb.

My husband sat next to me holding one hand, and our physician took my other hand. The physician waited patiently for us to take in the news that had just been shared. He again asked us if we had any questions, but we honestly couldn't even process what we had been told. After many minutes of silence, he continued. In a hesitant and creaking voice, the physician informed us that although he did not agree with it, the law afforded us the opportunity to end the pregnancy immediately should we so desire. It seemed like the air in the already heavy room, stood still. My heart knew the answer, and I had to trust that my husband would affirm the same belief. Psalm 139:13—"For you created my inmost being; you knit me together in my mother's womb"—echoed in my head. Without needing time for discussion or contemplation, my husband responded. He boldly stated that would not be an option for us.

As his words were spoken, you could feel the heaviness shift as a new hope filled the room. Our physician was ready and willing to support us in every way. Although terrified and quite shaken by the news, we were determined to fight for our baby. We understood that the diagnosis was serious and lacking promise, but I also knew that God had grabbed my attention in a mighty way and I was not going to back down on trusting in His ways and not my own. I had spent many years reading my Bible. I always found encouragement there, and I knew God had a bigger plan. I was then taken to another verse in my memory, Isaiah 55:8: "For my thoughts are not your thoughts, neither are your ways my ways." I had to trust that God knew exactly what his plan was and not look at what I was being told from a medical perspective.

Having stated our desires, the conversation shifted as our physician began to discuss our next steps. There was now a need to transition me to a higher level of care. I did not need to terminate my patient/physician relationship with him; however, he wanted to have further testing scheduled to get a complete diagnosis of the baby's condition. We were in agreement and excited to think that maybe further testing would provide light in this dark situation. Maybe, a higher level of care would give our baby a better chance. Prior to leaving our appointment that day, we sat with our scheduling team and set up an appointment with a specialty care team for the next morning. Completely aware that the diagnosis was grim, we left with an unexplainable hope that this next appointment would provide better direction and clarity regarding what we would be facing.

In this world you will have
trouble. But take heart! I
have overcome the world.
—John 16:33

Chapter *9*

F ollowing the appointment, we returned to our friends' home,
where our boys had spent the morning. Smiles and hugs welcomed us as we walked through the entry of their home, and
then appropriately following our welcome, the inquiry came—"How
did the appointment go?" Instantly, our hearts sank. In that moment,
we had to decipher our emotions, suddenly realizing that we were
not at all prepared to share our news. My husband simply responded,
"Not well." The smiles of our friends quickly shifted to expressions of
confusion and question. My husband is quite the jokester at times.
Although we knew this was not a situation where he was creating
humor, we could tell by the wandering eyes of our friend and her
young daughters that an explanation was warranted. Within seconds
of the inquiry, her husband joined us in the foyer. He too entered with
a beaming smile, only to be taken aback by the dismayed expressions
worn by each of us. It was then that we began to reveal the situation
as best we could. We explained that the test results we had received
that morning indicated that our baby did not have kidneys and that
the outcome following delivery was grim. Although we were trying
to answer their questions, we still had many of our own. As I stood
there processing how to respond, I also recognized a transition happening within me.

In those moments, I was able to experience first-hand the things
I had spent years seeking and searching for. In the past, as I faced
uncertainty, I knew fear, sorrow, pain, and confusion were upon me;

but in this moment, I was over taken by the ability to replace those emotions with an unexplainable strength and profound grace as faith was poured out upon us. As they took in our words of confusion and sadness, they simply responded by saying "Let us pray for you."

Growing up Catholic, I was familiar with prayer. As a child, I had been told that people had prayed for me. I personally had told people that I would pray for them. As I grew in my faith, I learned the importance of prayer—but in all of that learning, this moment was different. As we stood in the entry of their home, life became real; we stood there, not alone, but surrounded by peace, love, and grace. Without hesitation, no pomp and circumstance, no grand entry into the living room, we were taken just a few steps into their home, simply to the base of the staircase, and sat there to pray in a very real and loving environment. As we sat there, the staircase grew smaller and smaller as not only our adult friends desired to pray for us—their two preteen daughters, their son, and ours all came together in an instant to pray for our baby and for us.

As I reflect on various scriptures I have read over the years, I know that their example in that moment is exactly what Jesus would have done. "Come to me all you who are weary and burdened, and I will give you rest" (Matthew 11:28). As we sat there looking directly into the eye of a frightening storm ahead, we were covered in peace and ready to see what God had planned next. In the doctor's office that afternoon, we were hit with frightening news, yet within an hour, and after clarifying to our physician that our God was in control and our trust was in his plan, we found ourselves comforted and encouraged by this active prayer and support of friends. There was no hesitation, no preparation, just hearts joined together lifting up hope for a better outcome for our little one. I left there truly understanding how faith allows God's peace to break through life's storms.

The next morning, we woke and headed to the specialty clinic in anticipation of good news. We now had approximately twenty hours to take in the diagnosis and mentally and emotionally begin the process of accepting reality. As we drove, we pondered many things. In our minds, we understood the physical diagnosis—our baby did not have kidneys—and we knew there would be complications with this. We understood how this missing organ would affect urine production as well as prevent respiratory development; however, we were also considering that we lived in a great city. We knew we had one of the top children's hospitals in the country practically in our backyard. This knowledge gave us new reassurance as we prepared to fight this battle for our baby. We felt fortunate that we would have some of the best physicians potentially on our team.

We arrived at the office positive and hopeful. Perhaps this was an alternative way to deal with the anxiety that was surfacing, or maybe this was a way to protect ourselves emotionally, but we entered hopeful and highly anticipating clear goals for what the next step in our pregnancy would look like. The heaviness of the situation was lessened simply by knowing that in just a few moments, we would again have the opportunity to see our sweet baby on the monitor and hear its precious heartbeat.

As the technician began to turn monitors on and prepare equipment, I found myself amazed at the high-tech level of equipment that was available to us. There were such differences in this equipment from the original office ultrasounds we had been exposed to in both this and our previous pregnancies. In all previous ultrasounds, we had the privilege of viewing our baby on a black-and-white screen. This time, it was all in color. The technician carefully explained many things while she gathered her data. She informed us that the reflection of red and blue images represented blood flow to vital organs. We listened to her explanations while being drawn into this sweet, amazing little life before our eyes. Our baby appeared to be responding to the touch of the equipment by playfully twisting and turning as the ultrasound wand scanned over the baby. We sat, looking on in pure love as we were again united with our baby through the gift of technology. The breathtaking minutes ticked by, and then elation took over when the sounds of the room were overtaken with the steady, rigorous, beat of our precious baby's heart. My husband held my hand as we just took it in and listened.

This went on for quite a while before we noticed that the technician had been spending a considerable amount of time snapping pictures of one particular area. My husband asked her reasoning for this, and she gladly filled us in. Because of the specific diagnosis of renal agenesis (lack of kidney formation), the technician was gathering as much information as possible to either defend or reject the diagnosis. If there were no kidneys, there would also be a lack of blood vessels in that area as vital nutrition would not be needed. Through this regimen of picture taking, the technician commented that there was a "tiny trace" of possible blood flow in the area where a healthy kidney should be. Delight quickly stirred in our hearts. My husband immediately took this as an opportunity for humor and followed her comment with his order, "Keep looking. God just dropped it [the kidney] in there last night. It's too tiny to see it yet!" His comment brought a smile to everyone and increased our hope in the situation. The technician completed gathering the information that was necessary and escorted us into an office to wait on the physician.

It was only moments before we met the next physician on our growing list of medical professionals. She seemed eager to review the results and provide any support and information that would be helpful to us; unfortunately, her news proved no better than the previous day. Actually, she was able to dismiss all hope when she confirmed that there had been absolutely no right or left kidney formation in the early stages of our pregnancy. She also confirmed that there was nothing medically that could be done for our baby. With two healthy pregnancies down, we knew we were walking into unchartered waters. She provided us with plenty of time to ask questions and gave us an immeasurable amount of support. She then offered us her office for as long as we needed to reflect on the information and discuss anything we needed. She then stepped outside but assured us she would be available if we had any questions.

I sat there numb, processing the last few years of my life. I had walked many of my early years alone both physically and emotionally in an effort to protect myself. After so many losses as a child, I had chosen to push people away to reduce additional emotional hurt. I had spent many years mastering the art of seclusion and building walls of defense around my heart. In my efforts to be alone, I had perfected a balance between social living and safety. I had a good life, but I had also maintained my boundaries and protected myself from not allowing anyone to be too close. I did not want anyone to know the pain I had experienced, nor did I want to cause anyone to have pain. Now, in this life-changing moment, pain was starring me directly in the face, and I knew that in the past, running was my only option.

Hiding and running was my old coping mechanism built on fear and pain. It would be safe, and no one would know the depth of my agony. No one would see my tears or hear my lament. I would portray myself with strength while accepting the diagnosis, and I would play a convincing role of being content. I had lived this way for years and I knew that I could protect myself in this way. I could deal with this diagnosis alone and safe while pushing my husband away; or I could try something new and simply *trust*.

This was a new day. In that moment, I threw fear and pain aside, and I chose to reflect on the truths that I had searched so long for. It was time to put my faith into action and live—no more hiding. Scripture tells us in 2 Corinthians 5:17, "Therefore, if anyone is in Christ, he is a new creation: the old has gone, the new has come." In the past, I would feel defeat and anger when difficulties came my way. This time, I was feeling peace and encouragement. The difference in my life at this time was that I was not facing this alone or without hope. I had Christ in my life, and I did not have to take on this worldly trouble alone.

I reflected on the voice I had heard years back—the voice that called out to me, "It's time to walk alone"—and I knew that God was there guiding me and providing answers. Today was no different. This diagnosis may have seemed bizarre and messed up to me from a worldly perspective, but God had a heavenly perspective that had not been revealed to me yet. As I sat in the office with my husband by my side, I knew that I only had one choice. God had not let me down in the past. As I was seeking him, I realized that I had been learning how to trust as well. Trusting God never meant that life became perfect and easy, but life did become manageable and exciting. I did not know what was ahead, but I knew who held my future, and as I took in those moments to reflect on my past, I chose to continue the same pathway of trust for my future.

Without further hesitation, I looked my husband directly in his eyes. Somewhat terrified but also with an incredible amount of peace, I simply asked him, "Are you in this with me?" In that moment, I realized that I was truly choosing to walk alone, but ultimately, I was hoping he would come along. I was going to trust God with whatever obstacles came at me and my baby, and I was not going to hide. In that moment, I tore down my safety nets. No more running; no more stuffing my feelings. I had to make a choice. Outwardly, the choice seemed to be between my husband and myself. Would we accept this worldly trial together? But inwardly, I knew the choice was so much more. Inwardly, I faced a pivotal faith moment. Would I be able to trust in the God that I had been seeking all these years? Would I allow him to walk me through this, and would he prove faithful no matter what the outcome was? In that moment of choice, no time was needed for decision-making. My husband, mirroring my deep look into his eyes, quickly answered my question with a simple "Yes."

I don't know if there are words to describe that moment. To this day, my eyes well up with tears when I think of the heart victory that was won that day. We sat in the office and just held each-other. The joy that I was feeling seemed so twisted considering what we were facing, but I knew that we were not facing anything alone, and the peace that surrounded us was immense. Although I knew that I had no idea what was coming, I also knew that I had hope in the one who knew every detail, and that was all I needed. God had a plan, and my job was to simply trust in it.

Consider it pure joy, my brothers, whenever you face trials of many kinds, because you know that the testing of your faith develops perseverance.
—James 1:2–3

Chapter 10

Following that appointment, our life again returned to normal—at least, what our new normal would be. As we continued to face the reality of our diagnosis, our prayers became focused around our hope for complete healing for our baby—if that was God's will. Believing that God is a God of joy, we wanted to do everything possible to be joyful in this trial. God had given us our sweet baby, and only he knew what would come in the future. We had made the choice to trust in God's plan, and we wanted joy to surround us during this trial. Because of this, we had decided not to share our diagnosis with many people. We wished to keep our hope alive; however, our plan to shelter our family did not work. The select friends that we chose to tell also ended up sharing our news with others. We knew word had spread only from pure hearts and their true intention to obtain more opportunity for prayer. We soon learned that our initial, minor list of people whom we wished to include had multiplied quickly, and the result, although all were heartfelt, was both an encouragement as well as a disappointment.

Although word was spreading vastly among friends within our church, our immediate family was still unaware of our diagnosis. My husband felt pushed to share with his mother, and I understood his desire. We hoped that she would be an additional encouragement and support as we walked this unfamiliar terrain. As expected, she was devastated at the news and just as confused as we had been. She was supportive while we stood with her in her kitchen, but then shortly after we left, whether she was driven by curiosity or confusion, she decided the Internet would be a good resource. Later, after she had gathered various bits of information, she called my husband and shared with him additional gut-wrenching details pertaining to babies born with this condition. She filled him in on all the physical deformities they could have and reinforced that death from complications, according to the Internet, was the only result. When my husband shared this with me, I was crushed. She was a Christian and a mother herself. We had tried to keep our circle of support filled with people that would bring us wisdom, support, and love. I felt betrayed, but I also knew that betrayal was not from God. Although I was hurt by her actions, I personally decided to pray for her and my relationship with her over the next few weeks. In response to my prayer, I could see that God again was using this as a teaching moment. I recognized a clear distinction between seeking truth through scripture and seeking answers in this world. I also realized that we were not the only ones hurting through our baby's diagnosis. I recognized that each person is free to process difficulties in their own way. Through this, my husband and I were given strength to take the pain that her actions brought and transform it into wisdom and deeper knowledge of how to love others.

Our growing strength and peace did not come from our prayers alone. In contrast to the hurt that we felt from some, the support we received from our church family and dear friends far exceeded anything we could have imagined. The spreading news of our situation ignited a chain of support as we began receiving cards and phone calls of love and encouragement. One of the phone calls we received was from a church member who expressed a desire to come to our home and pray for us as well as anoint us with oil. Although I had heard about this in the Christian Church, the concept on a personal level was completely new to me. I had to reflect back on what I knew as a Catholic to even accept the idea.

In the Catholic faith, babies are anointed with oil at baptism, and I believe there are other times the faith uses oil, but I am not familiar enough with it to list those. As I reflected on my Catholic upbringing, I came to a place where I was not afraid of the idea. In addition, I had done enough personal research in the Christian faith, and I knew that I trusted these friends. Finally, I found support in my Bible as I read James 5:14–15, "Is any one of you sick? He should call the elders of the church to pray over him and anoint him with oil in the name of the Lord. And the prayer offered in faith will make the sick person well." I talked with my husband, and we chose to embrace their sweet request to try and help us in a deeply spiritual way. It was only a few days later that a small group of friends, with hearts dedicated to prayer, came into our home and prayed with us as well as anointing our heads with oil. As I had said, this was nothing that I had experienced in the past, but it gave us yet another tiny burst of hope for our baby's future.

That sweet time together was not just a time to sit in silence and listen to their prayers, but it also provided us time to talk openly about our situation. Life had been busy since our diagnosis, and this may have been one of the first conversations my husband and I had had with other faith-believing adults since the day we had received the dreadful news. It was greatly welcomed. In that time of sharing, my husband began to open up emotionally. He shared that as he realized the future was uncertain, he felt that if our baby was going to need to live on machines, he would rather God take the baby now, rather than see it suffer. I had not heard those words from him up to this point. The reality of what he was saying was difficult to hear; however, I remained at peace. I knew God was in control, and I was trusting in His plan. Our friends listened to our hearts and again prayed with us. The evening was peaceful and ended with a feeling of more encouragement knowing that we were not walking through this journey alone.

During the next few weeks, we continued to encounter great support as well as surprising disappointments. I recall one afternoon when I had gone over to my in-laws. I was standing in the kitchen when my father-in-law approached me and asked how I was. My response to his questions included a reference to how much the baby was kicking and moving around. His facial expression was one of complete shock, which also matched his verbal tone when he commented, "You can feel the baby move?" The comment caught me by surprise and with great pain; however, I was able to pull strength from within me and simply respond, "Of course I can!" Weeks had passed since our diagnosis, but our baby was alive and well. Through the difficulties of the diagnosis, I was choosing to enjoy my pregnancy and carry the hope that healing was coming. I realized that he was looking at the pregnancy from worldly eyes, which can be devastating, but I found peace in reflecting on God's words: "For you created my inmost being; you knit me together in my mother's womb" (Psalm 139:13). I walked away reminded that this baby had a purpose and a plan, written by God, that simply had not yet been revealed to me.

As more and more time passed, it was obvious that a vast amount of people had become aware of our baby's health concern. In all of this, I continued to put my faith first. I continued to attend my weekly Bible study, serve at our church, have my own personal time to read my Bible, and seek out prayer from others. Each doctor's appointment was treasurable as we had the opportunity to listen to the precious rhythmic beat of our little one's heart. Our physician never rushed through our appointments, and he allowed us to take in every heartbeat that we desired to hear. It was a comfort to be able to go to him and be treated as an expectant mom, fully knowing that he was aware of the diagnosis yet allowing us to have the hope that we needed in the situation. As with any normal pregnancy, our office visits did not require further ultrasound in the progressive weeks of the pregnancy, which eliminated further discussion of a potential gender reveal. We continued to feel comfortable with our physician, but also never felt a need to share my kitchen experience with him. He always brought a strong understanding of the medical condition of our baby, yet he was completely unaware of the spiritual revelation I had experienced in regards to our baby's gender.

Although in a small way, I still questioned what I had experienced, in my heart I was filled with joy knowing secretly that I would have a daughter. As I had worked through my faith and pulled together my life after my mom's death, God had continued to strategically place strong women in my life. For a few years prior to this pregnancy, my eyes had been opened to the true beauty that a mother-daughter relationship was meant to be. I had many Christian friends who were raising daughters, and I witnessed beautiful mother-daughter friendships emerging. I had never experienced that level of intimacy with my mom. As time passed, I was able to break down the lies I had believed regarding poor relationships between mothers and daughters. I was able to replace them with the godly examples of what his true intention was for these treasured bonds.

Although we had shared our diagnosis with others, when it came to hearing Rose's name in our kitchen, my husband and I had chosen to keep that part of our story between us. I believe this was mostly my decision, and it was honestly based on human doubt. I knew what I had heard weeks earlier, alone in my kitchen. I knew that my husband was on board and fully supportive. However, I also knew that people were not as understanding. I had experienced it directly in the doubt of some of our family and friends as we shared the news about our baby. Truly, I also questioned myself and at times found myself asking if God really had spoken to me. But as I walked through this trial, I felt blessed that I did have friends with deep faith who continued to encourage my spiritual growth. I came to a point where I decided that I was ready to share.

Being a homeschool mom, I looked forward to the homeschool convention every year. Obviously I am a person who thrives off of learning new things, and I enjoy the drive of diving deep into a topic. My faith has followed the same pattern. The homeschool convention of 2005 was no different. Not only was I looking forward to the event from an academic standpoint, but socially I knew that I would be meeting with other supportive homeschool moms as well. The convention is always scheduled to run over a weekend. On this particular year, some girlfriends and I had decided to get a hotel and take advantage of some time to catch up, without little ones running around or the demands of laundry calling our names. After the convention came to a close on Friday night, we found ourselves kicked back and resting our feet in our hotel room. It was such a blessing to be surrounded by dear friends while attaining updates on all the families represented there. Sitting in the room, laughing and relaxing with friends, I felt led to share my kitchen experience. At first, I remember feeling nervous. What will these friends think of me? Will they even believe that this was true? But as I shared the story, I became more calm and confident in my words as I recapped the event.

After telling all of the details and watching their expressions, I felt my story was received well, but I did not honestly know to what level there was any belief in it. Certainly, no one questioned my sincerity and truth in the matter; however, I believe there was some doubt as to if I really had heard God's voice. I understood, because I too was thinking these same thoughts. However, I also knew that when I heard what I did, I felt God's peace. I knew I had experienced some intense yet peaceful emotion that I had not allowed myself to feel in years. I wanted the same response that I had received from my husband, but that did not happen. I knew they had their doubts, but the joy that filled me when I reflected on the experience could not be denied. I knew that in time, all doubt would be washed away.

Where, O death, is your victory?
Where, O death, is your sting?
  —1 Corinthians 15:55

Chapter *11*

The next few weeks were uneventful from a pregnancy stand-point and eventually led up to our next scheduled routine appointment. It was Wednesday, April 6, 2005. As scheduled and on time, we arrived for our appointment and customarily were then escorted into the exam room. The physician came in after only a short wait, carrying his Doppler instrument, which would enable us to listen to our baby. After a cordial exchange of greetings, our voices were replaced with the quick and musical rhythm of our baby's heartbeat. Following his traditional character, our physician granted us as much time as we felt necessary to rest and enjoy the repetitive sound of sweet perfection that then filled the room. During that time, we shared friendly conversation with the physician and listened peacefully to the rhythm. Finally, without new health concerns or questions on our minds, we finished the appointment and headed home. The peace that filled our hearts from having heard our little one's heartbeat carried us through our routine evening plans and the busy schedule planned for the following day.

The next evening, April 7, concluded as it almost always did: I scurried around the house gathering toys, clothes, and dishes from a long and successful day. At one point, while I was working to find closure to the day, I felt my baby give a fierce, attention-grabbing kick. The movement was not uncommon as I had experienced high activity levels the entire pregnancy, but this kick was significantly different. I believe my baby wanted my attention, and he or she got it. Immediately, I reached for my belly and caressed the area where I felt the kick. With a smile on my face and contentment in my heart, I continued to work around the house until finally I had grown exhausted and decided to get ready for bed. It wasn't until I had laid my head down on my pillow that I had realized that the large kick I had felt earlier was the last one I remembered feeling throughout the night. I knew that I had had a long day, and I was tired. I also knew that babies toss and turn until they wear themselves out as well. This thought brought me comfort, and I was able to rest peacefully knowing that my baby and I had had a fulfilling yet exhausting day.

The next morning came early, as Fridays always did. For approximately a year and a half, I had been meeting every Friday morning with three strong Christian women. Considering that my children were the youngest in our group, we would gather in my home and enjoy time encouraging each other. Some weeks were filled with reading and discussing scripture together, other weeks we would discuss a particular book that we had chosen to read together, and at other times we would find encouragement and support simply by sharing life experiences. I had grown to look forward to my girl time and this particular Friday was no different. I was eager to start my day, however, I couldn't help but reflect on the fact that I had not been awakened during the night by the baby moving and kicking about. As I had done before going to sleep, I comforted myself remembering that sometimes my baby wakes as I get moving in the morning. With this thought on my mind, I got up and prepared for my friends to arrive.

Our regular routine called for us to meet around six in the morning. I do not recall what type of conversation we had that week, but I know that I felt thankful that we were together. I always felt encouraged and challenged at the end of our meetings. I do not know what I had done to deserve such amazing, God-fearing women in my life, but I knew what a treasure I had been given. After our meetings each week, we would close our time together with prayer.

On this morning, as my turn for prayer requests came around, I simply commented that I had not felt the baby moving, and I asked for prayer for that concern. Each of these women were aware of our diagnosis and immediately spoke words of encouragement and reassurance prior to praying. Their sweet words comforted me as a million thoughts were spinning in my head. While they were praying, my uncertainty was transformed into an unwavering peace in my heart. I knew that everything was going to be all right, because I knew who already held all the answers. I looked up at my friends following prayer and said, "I'm certain this is different." Quickly, they offered more reassurance, not wanting to face the possibility that something had happened. They encouraged me to make a call to the doctor immediately just to be sure. As we concluded our group, one of my friends let me know that she was available if I needed help with the other kids. On that particular day, not only did I have my two boys, but I had taken on babysitting for two little girls as well. My friend indicated she would be willing to watch all of the kids for me if needed. I thanked her and she left.

The little girls arrived just as my friends were leaving, as they usually did, and soon after that, I was able to make my call to the doctor, as it was finally 8:00 a.m. The response to come to the office as soon as possible was a little surprising, but I followed his orders. Immediately following my call to the physician, I made two more calls: one to my friend to have her return to my house and one to my husband. Both responded quickly, and before I knew it, my husband and I were heading off to the doctor once again—we had just been there two days prior.

As soon as we arrived at the doctor's office, we were taken into a room and evaluated by ultrasound. Although my heart knew the truth, my mind waited expectantly. I held on to the hope that I would catch a glimpse of our sweet little angel wiggling and squirming around. I listened intently, longing to celebrate the sound of a fluttering heartbeat. That moment did not come. With a heavy sigh, our physician confirmed that there was no heartbeat and that our baby had passed. The already heavy room grew even more eerily silent. The physician spoke to us briefly and offered his condolences. Then he gave us some time to be alone. For the second time in just about a month, my husband and I found ourselves numb and alone in a physician's office; the only response we had for each other was to hold each other close. In those short moments, we experienced tears and sadness, but overall, there was peace—a peace that simply could not be explained. Together, we rested in that comfort.

After a short time, our physician returned. He asked us what our thoughts were, and we explained that we had some celebrations planned for that evening as well as the next day. My dear friend, one of my Friday-morning accountability girls, was turning forty, and I had been helping to plan a surprise birthday party for her. The party was scheduled for that night. In addition, our oldest son would be turning ten, and we had planned his first overnight birthday party for the following night. We explained to our physician that it was our goal to celebrate a couple of people we dearly loved and we did not want to selfishly dampen their celebrations with crushing news. Our physician responded by assuring that my health was not at risk should I decide to carry our baby during the events. He understood the pain that went along with the news he had just shared with us and encouraged us to celebrate if that would help us. After a short discussion, we decided that we would continue with plans to celebrate our friend and our son, and after our celebrations, we would meet our physician to deliver our baby on Sunday.

Following our appointment, we returned home, where my friend was watching our boys and the extra girls. On our way home, we had decided not to tell our boys the news just yet, or anyone for that matter. We had a weekend of celebrations ahead, and that was what we wanted our focus to be. We were not denying our situation, but our desire was to celebrate the friends and son that we had already been given. When we arrived home, I contacted the parents of the little girls and asked them to pick the kids up, which they each were able to do quickly. We chose to tell my friend who was staying with our boys, and she offered to take both of our boys to her house for the day. This was a wonderful gift to us and would allow us the time that we needed to process our emotions.

Once all of the kids were taken care of, my husband and I decided we would need something to eat to give us fuel to get through the day. We found ourselves at a local sub shop and placed our order. As we waited on our food, I looked around at the serving counter. It was filled with photos of past customers giving thumbs-up and accolades for an enjoyable meal. As I followed the string of photos down the counter, I unexpectedly came across an ultrasound photo hanging in the mix. This picture had a memo added across the front which read "Future sub lover." Reading this brought me to tears and immediately eliminated my appetite. The peace I had felt was still with me, but I also felt a little bit of anger and felt slightly sick to my stomach. I knew I had actively chosen to trust God through this no matter what bumps would surface while on the journey. Although this was not the outcome I was hoping for, I fully trusted God. He was faithful, and I was going to be as well. This was a difficult, gut-wrenching experience, but I was not going to go back on my word and commitment to my faith.

Over our lunch, as we attempted to pull together our emotions, my husband and I shared conversation regarding what the rest of the day would look like. The only true thing on our agenda was to pick up the cake for the surprise party, yet in the simplicity of that plan, my heart was stirring. I sat there empty, with my best friend across the table. I was longing for something but unsure what that void was. My heart was broken. I was realizing the depth of what had occurred, and I longed for my baby. I asked my husband if we could run to a local baby store and purchase outfits for our little one. With all that had happened thus far in our pregnancy, we had not yet begun to decorate a nursery, pick out color themes, or even think about clothing. As a mom, I had been joyfully awaiting the day I would hold this new life, look at its precious face, and begin to meet all of its needs, but this was not the plan for our little one. As I sat there, I began to feel comfort in knowing that I could still find the perfect outfit, dress my baby, and hold and adore my little one once we delivered. My husband was in agreement, and this plan gave us purpose in our time of grief, so off to the baby store we headed.

When we arrived at the baby store, we walked directly to the clothing section. We still had not confirmed, from a medical standpoint, if our baby was a boy or a girl. As we approached the clothing department, I had two requests for my husband. First, I asked that the preemie outfits we chose (boy and girl) would both include a bonnet to cover our baby's head. In addition, I asked my husband if I could choose the outfit for a girl, and if he would be willing to choose one for a boy. He was in agreement. He went and found the sweetest light blue pantsuit outfit with a light blue bonnet. I also went looking and retrieved a light pink two-piece outfit, also with a bonnet. My outfit was accented with dainty rose blossoms scattered throughout the light pink material. Completing this step in our grief process brought both a sense of fulfillment as well as a deep sadness as we realized this would be the only purchase we would have to make. We simply held each other in the aisle, taking in the moment until we had enough strength to walk hand-in-hand up to the checkout counter.

The day seemed to have flown by although we really had not accomplished much. Most importantly, we were together and able to share countless moments of holding each other and shedding tears. During our time, we made plans and talked about how we would tell our friends and family. It was a difficult day, but one where our hearts were able to draw nearer to one another. As I walked through each step of that day, I continued to feel pain, but also great peace. The only way I can explain that contrast is to reflect on scripture. Matthew 11:28 says, "Come to me, all you who are weary and burdened, and I will give you rest." I knew that as I drew near to God in my pain, he was providing the peace that I was feeling and giving me the strength I needed to get through the day. Once the shopping was complete, it was time to pick up the cake and head toward the location of the surprise party. I found it a blessing to have the opportunity to share a joyful event in the midst of such a painful one. I knew it would be a difficult night with many emotions; however, it was one where we also would be surrounded by the love of our friends. Soon we were at the party location and pulling together the final details. Our excitement was on the joy of the surprise to come, and not on the pain of our situation. We felt relieved that we had kept our secret and our night would be focused on the celebration for our friend.

As the guests arrived, you could feel the house fill with excitement and anticipation. All of our efforts proved to be successful when the birthday girl walked into the room and complete shock covered her face as she was welcomed with the ear-piercing shout of "Surprise!" Applause, greetings with hugs, and well wishes were given throughout the room. It was a moment of elation that was most desperately needed in my heart, and I took in the joy of celebrating what a wonderful friend I had been given.

Soon after, when the initial welcome had calmed down, I was approached by the birthday girl and another friend; both of these women were in my Friday-morning group. I had intentionally not called either one after our visit to the doctor that morning— not to harm them, but to have time with my husband and think through our plans. They lovingly cornered me and asked how my appointment went. Caught off guard, I simply smiled and answered, "Everything is good." Apparently I was not very good at covering it up. They both looked right through me and asked more detailed questions. I knew that I had to be transparent with them, so I pulled them aside to have the first of many difficult conversations. "We lost the baby" was all I had to say. I can't really explain it, but when the words came from my mouth, I became stronger than I had been all day. I was able to comfort my friends as they broke down and processed the news. I was able to be an encouragement and support to them in a way that no person going through this type of loss should have been able to do on their own. I know that God was giving me strength in my weakness, and I was able to care for them in that moment. I filled them in on what our day had looked like and our plans to deliver the baby on Sunday. When all the details were out and we had pulled ourselves together, I firmly stated that for now we had an amazing woman to celebrate and it was time to get back to the party. We did just that.

A time to weep and a time
to laugh, a time to mourn
and a time to dance.
—Ecclesiastes 3:4

Chapter 12

T he next day was Saturday, April 9. Our son woke with excitement knowing it was his big day—his first sleepover as he was about to turn ten years old! We spent the day preparing food, setting up games, and decorating. Friends and family began to arrive early in the afternoon, and the party was off to a great start on a beautiful spring day. The celebrations carried on until dusk where the party moved inside for some intense dodgeball competition. I chose to step out of this activity as it was late and I just didn't want to get pummeled by boys being boys. I took the opportunity to spend some quality time with my sister who had driven in from another state.

Prior to the evening coming upon us, I had found my sister and me working seamlessly to put together all the details to make the party a success. As we had worked diligently throughout the day, I found myself reflecting on our past as sisters. At one point, she was my best friend, but the pain of our parents' losses had created an emotional gap over the years. I would do anything for my sister, and I knew my sister would do anything for me, but heartache can cause severe damage to relationships. As young children, we had no idea how to handle our pain, so stuffing it and hiding from reality was the best we could do. We could get together for any celebration, but when it came to sharing emotion, I could not remember back far enough to any time where that was comfortable. The only emotion I could recall in the years that had passed between us was anger, and unfortunately, I was the one typically lashing out. Over the years, we had worked through conflict, but we had not taken our relationship deep. Now, having walked in my faith for multiple years and allowing God to do a work in my heart, I desired more. I knew that God had rewired my heart. I knew that I was able to deal with tears and emotion now in a way I never had, and most importantly, I knew that I had a treasure in my sister and that I needed her in that moment more than I ever had before.

I recognized that this was another turning point for me. As tradition of my past had played out, I could run, share only a little with her and keep the rest locked up inside, but it was time for me to let my past go. It was time for God to do exactly what he had planned, and I was willing to take the ride. I knew that I had to open up to her. I knew that deep emotions would surface as I let her know what was going on with my baby. I was used to hiding, especially from her. Anger was much easier for me than walking through grief. In the past, I refused to let her see me as anything but strong (emotionally as well as physically), but in this grieving process, I was realizing that this was not just about me.

We sat on the couch together, and I simply told her that I had something that I needed to share. She sat quietly yet inquisitively and waited. My heart was racing. I sat facing my sister knowing I had such a difficult thing to tell her, but I also knew that I hadn't let myself truly open up to her emotionally in as long as I could remember. Eighteen years had passed since we lost our dad. Eighteen years of growing up wanting to have my best friend back but not wanting—or not knowing how—to share my hurt.

I saw this as a moment of strength and a new opportunity—the opportunity to simply be real. I had an opportunity to share my faith with her in this moment while also sharing the pain that would come with my news. I knew my words, my tone, and my delivery of the message was most important to allow her to hear me and see my heart. I did not want her to see the pain that had dominated my heart in the past when I was running my life. I was different, and I knew why. This was my opportunity to share with her and model for her what choosing love through pain looked like. I was no longer that angry, emotionless sister, but one filled with grace. I wanted her to know that what I was facing was difficult, but that through the love of Christ, I was pulling through with his strength, when I humanly had no strength left. I was ready to make a stand for my heavenly Father and show her what it meant to truly live for Christ; something we had never experienced in the Catholic faith. Without drawing it out or trying to make the words easier to swallow, I simply told her that we had lost the baby.

As the words crossed my lips, the tears immediately poured down my cheeks. I had been so strong at the doctor; reality began to sink in during the time with my husband; and I had celebrated with wonderful friends at the party. Sitting there, hearing the words come from my mouth and looking directly into her eyes, I burst emotionally. I couldn't stop the tears, and as I cried, she cried with me. I realized as we sat there together that this was the first true cry we had had together in many years. The loss of my child was devastating; however, sitting with my sister and sharing this pain from a godly heart somehow allowed me to open up another locked portion of my heart. I believe the tears that were being shed at that time, also included tears from many years back, when we had to say good-bye to our father, but did not know how to work through that as young children. In addition, I couldn't help but think that they also included the pain of the loss of our mother. We were a bit older in that loss, but still too young to know how to process the grief. For the first time in my life, I fully opened up to her emotionally. The trust that sisters are to share suddenly returned to my heart, and I felt overwhelmed that God had given me such a treasure in her. I wish I had been sitting there, sharing any number of other topics with her, but I know that in that moment, God was at work again, using my pregnancy to remove another layer from my tightly sealed heart.

I realized that God had given me tears, not only for the loss of my baby, but for the pain that I had been carrying for so very long. I thought that I had to be the one to hold my life together. I thought that I had hidden it all so well—pushed it away and in my own way dealt with all the things that I needed to deal with. But reality was, I was just beginning to let it all go. As I sat there with my sister, I knew that the tears we shared in that moment were tears of love, tears of support, tears of sadness, tears of fear, and tears of joy—joy for the new beginning I would have with her—and I stayed in that moment for a time, taking it all in.

Eventually, I turned the conversation from tears to my next step: I was going to need more help. I had a room full of boys celebrating my son's birthday. There was an abundant amount of laughter coming from the basement, but in the morning, I had to pack up all the boys and be ready to head to church to meet their families. I knew that emotions would most likely be hitting us hard in the morning, as it was the Sunday we had told our physician we would meet for the delivery. I needed loving support, and I knew I could count on my sister to be that support, and she did not disappoint. The next morning, with the help of my husband and sister, we pulled together and successfully got everyone ready—including ourselves with bags packed for the hospital.

When we arrived at church, we were able to quickly return all of the kids to their parents. Next, we placed our youngest son in his preschool class, and then took our older son into service with us. Our plan was to attend the worship portion of the service and then dismiss ourselves along with our oldest son to a quiet room in the church office where we would tell him the news about the baby. We had a plan, but we had no idea that God had already put a twist into it.

We had attended the same church for more than ten years and, for the most part, had always had the same worship pastor. Unfortunately, the previous summer, our favorite worship pastor had accepted a position at a church out of state, and we had sadly said goodbye to him and his family months prior to that particular Sunday. I believe this amazing friend and worship pastor was a large reason why our oldest son carried such a passion for music. Over the years, we had spent many hours attending night of worship sessions with our worship pastor, Mr. Matt leading us. In addition, as our friendship grew, we had spent time in his home, and they in ours as well. They were strong, God-loving people, and we were blessed to have them in our lives. We had kept in touch after their move out of state that summer, but we had no idea that they were in town on this particular weekend. It was a wonderful surprise when worship opened on that Sunday morning and our Mr. Matt unexpectedly took the stage to lead us! What an unforeseen blessing from God! Although we were about to share the most difficult news with our son, God had gone ahead of us and planted a blessing in our path. There is no way to describe the feelings I had at that time. All I could do was simply take it all in and recognize God's control. Not only was he carrying me through, but he was also providing for and loving my son as well.

After a wonderful worship set, we followed our plan and took our oldest son into the church office. I remember sitting there, before anyone started talking, and having a flashback to my early days sitting in a school office ready to hear bad news, and here I was again. A circle of support surrounded us as we had immediately been joined by close friends and their son (who had been best friends with our son for more than eight years now). I sat in an all-too-familiar setting again, waiting for devastating news to be shared. This time, it was myself in the role of sharing the difficult news and my son in the role of waiting to hear. Although the memories that this situation brought back to me were painful, the peace that surrounded this meeting was unquestionable.

My husband and I took a seat across from our son. Certain that this was the most difficult conversation a father could have with his son, my husband handled it boldly. He reminded our son about how we had been asking God to heal the baby if that was his will. Our son listened with great interest and respect. Then my husband proceeded to tell our son that God decided not to heal the baby and that the baby had gone to heaven. His eyes welled up with tears along with everyone else's in the room. Without hesitation, our son's ten-year-old friend wrapped his arms around our son, and together they cried. I could not have prepared my son for what he was about to hear. As a mother, you want to always protect your children and block them from hurt and pain, but I am powerless to do that in every situation. In that moment, when I could not protect him, I was able to witness the sweetest reflection of God's purest love as these ten-year-old boys comforted each other. This was not a situation any parent should have to be in, and we did not know what proper protocol looked like, so we just let the boys handle things as they happened naturally.

Shortly after the shock of the news had worn off, our son's best friend then broke the silence by informing our son that the arrangement was to stay at his friends' house for a few days. Both of the boys perked up and conversation transitioned to making plans, which included building action figures and racing cars together. Scripture says, "I will turn their mourning into gladness: I will give them comfort and joy instead of sorrow" (Jeremiah 31:13). We witnessed God doing just that in this precious friendship.

Up to this point, and even through the last few days of the weekend, I had been making it through by focusing on the action that was needed next. After telling our son, I continued on my path by ensuring car seats were moved into my friend's van and overnight bags for the boys were transferred as well. I kept busy and tried my best to avoid conversation with the many friends whom we had seen in church that morning. I was not in any place to plan out what the next part of my day would look like, nor did I really know. What I knew was that my boys were taken care of and I was scheduled to meet my doctor at noon. With that knowledge, I pushed forward and completed packing the boys in the car and gave them our hugs goodbye. This moment trumped all of the difficult obstacles I had faced in the last forty-eight hours. There I was, sending my healthy boys off, promising they would be well taken care and with the hopes of much fun to be had fully knowing that this was the last task to keep me busy before the delivery. After passing as much love as I could on to the boys, my husband and I walked hand in hand to our vehicle to begin the final leg of the journey to the hospital.

Although we had been through the childbirth process in the past, this was a whole new endeavor. We did not know what was going to take place, but we found peace in knowing fully that God already had it all lined up. "'For I know the plans I have for you,' declares the Lord, 'plans to prosper you and not to harm you, plans to give you hope and a future'" (Jeremiah 29:11).

As we drove to the hospital, I couldn't help but wonder what God was possibly doing. I couldn't help but to focus on various scripture that had come to mind. The first one was where Jesus had welcomed Lazarus back to life (John 11:38–44), then I thought of the little girl who had died and Jesus brought her back to life (Mark 5:21–43), and finally, the blind man whose sight Jesus had restored (Luke 18:35–43). In each of these miracles, I knew that it was pure faith that Jesus acted upon. This is exactly what I had been in search of all of my life. I wanted a faith that was real, and in my searching, I was sure that I had found just that. I knew that I was nothing special, but I also knew that doubt would take me down the path to nowhere, and hope would bring me a full and abundant life, so I moved forward with the hope that God was going to do something really big. In the past, through heartache and loss, I chose anger and withdrawal, but in this moment, I refused to turn back to my old ways. Again, I was taken to a scripture that I had memorized: "But now, Lord, what do I look for? My hope is in you" (Psalm 39:7). I was able to look at my fear and transform it into strength, knowing God already had the details worked out, and I just had to walk through the storm.

Find rest, O my soul,
in God alone; my hope
comes from him.
—Psalm 62:5

Chapter *13*

When we arrived at the hospital, we were welcomed and quickly set up in our room. Paperwork was completed, and the traditional medical procedures were followed. Everything moved along like clockwork as I actively participated externally. Internally, faith and hope were the only defenses I had.

The medical tasks at hand became my new distraction. Historically, I have always opted for natural childbirth, and this baby was not getting any exception. Physically, my body was not ready to deliver by any means, so the doctors had to initiate a plan to begin the labor process. Traditionally, this would be through the means of intravenous (IV) medications; however, I was not in agreement with a medicated delivery. Following my birth plan, it was agreed to administer oral medications to induce my labor. We were told that this process could take much longer than with the use of the IV medications, which allowed us to recognize the need to sit back, reflect, talk, and prepare for what the next few hours may look like. Fortunately, for my husband, it happened to be the week of the Masters Golf Tournament, so he quickly (after checking with me and meeting my needs) turned on the tournament and became engaged in the play.

Once my admission was complete and we were settled, we took time to pray together and share our feelings. We were as ready as we could be and willing to let God work his plan through our lives. It was not long after our admission was complete that our physician entered the room. He arrived dressed in street clothes and indicated that he had just finished enjoying lunch with his son. He knew that I would not be anywhere near delivery, but he added that he was simply there because he wanted to check in on us. This blew me away. He did not have to be there at all. In the first place, he had told us when we were in the office that past Friday that he was not on call that weekend, but that he wished to deliver our baby for us regardless. I could not have imagined delivering with any other physician, and we accepted his offer at that time. This physician had delivered my first two babies, and I was quickly realizing that my meeting him so many years ago was also another part of God's big plan to bring blessings to my life, even in difficult times. Second, he came in as a friend reaching out in a difficult situation. Although most of the focus was on preparing me for delivery, my husband was going through this process and loss as well. A friend was exactly what my husband needed at the time, and that was what God had provided. For the next hour or so, my husband and my physician sat together and enjoyed the Master's Golf Tournament. As I sat waiting for the medications to begin producing contractions, I found peace in another verse that I had learned: "And my God will meet all your needs according to the riches of his glory in Christ Jesus" (Philippians 4:19). It blew me away to think that God would provide such a unique friend for my husband in such an unexpected way.

Eventually, our physician prepared to leave and reassured us that he would return for the delivery. He answered a few more of my questions and then excused himself. I had been resting in bed during the visit and wanted to get up and walk, so my husband and I began a short and uneventful walk around the maternity unit. Following our walk, we accepted a visit from our dear friends, which greatly helped to pass the time. During our visit, we were able to talk about how the boys were doing and felt a high level of support. They explained to us that they had set up a prayer chain that would continue throughout our delivery. Emotionally and spiritually, I knew that I was not walking through this journey alone. Physically, I could no longer ignore my contractions, but I was able to tolerate them. With the onset of each contraction, I would experience cold chills, and I tried to focus on anything but the pain and shivering. Our friends had been through four deliveries of their own, so they were fully aware of the subtle signs I was showing. They decided it was time to end the visit but not before asking if they could pray for us. Of course, we would not turn that down.

Although I cannot recall the exact words they prayed that evening, I do know their words were precisely what I needed to hear at that time. As they prayed, I trembled. I knew I had been experiencing cold chills, and I was certain that was what was continuing. When the prayer was complete, I thanked them and asked for a blanket, expressing how cold I felt. They looked at me quite surprised and simultaneously told me that while they were praying with me with their hands placed on my shoulders, they felt nothing but heat pouring from me. Biblically, these friends are recognized as sound, scholarly Bible teachers in our community. They assured me that this warmth was a representation of the presence of the Holy Spirit in my midst. Although discussion on the works of the Holy Spirit was a new experience for me, I was certain of my faith and trusting of their spiritual knowledge. I was willing to listen to them with no doubts. For whatever reason, I knew that as they left me that evening, although I had no further clarification of what God was doing, I was certain that it was all going to be OK. I hugged each of them as they prepared to leave and expressed my gratitude for all they were doing to love and support me through this difficult time.

Once again, after this visit, I decided it was time to get up and get moving. Together, my husband and I began walking the hallways a second time. Our conversation covered the journey we had been on and how quickly time had flown from the moment of diagnosis to delivery day. I still did not know why God had chosen us. I did not know what the next chapter in the story would be, but I knew that each contraction was another step closer to the end of this journey.

As we walked, I began to replay everything that had happened through the duration of my pregnancy. First, was the prayer that my friend was adamant to pray with me back in December. Then was the name I had heard God audibly speak to me in January. The diagnosis came in March, the prayers in our home after that, the extensive testing, and finally the hope that I was determined to carry. I walked and reflected on it all. An emotional hurricane was building up within me. I had experienced so much. I had been on this faith journey much longer than this pregnancy journey had been. I felt like for the first time in my life, I had answers. I thought that I was on the right path spiritually and I had found many friends who were sound in biblical truth that would support and encourage me along my walk. I took in all of these thoughts and tried to be strong. I tried to walk through every step of our diagnosis without doubting, but I truly did not know how God was going to write the last chapter of our story. Finally, while walking, I said to my husband, "If this isn't a girl, I am going to have to walk away from the church and everything I believe."

I knew that I had tried to live these last weeks as a testimony— the person I was in my distant past was no longer. This battle would be victorious because this time, I was walking with Christ. This time, my focus was not on bottling up my pain and pretending I was OK, but rather my focus was on knowing that he had a plan and a purpose and I had chosen to trust him. What was going to happen in the next few hours would define where I would go with my faith. Would there be a miracle in this delivery? Would there be a baby girl or a baby boy to cherish? I had no idea. I was waiting in limbo, but I was certain of one thing. I was either going to be in a situation where I would have a testimony to my faith or a situation where I would be revisiting all the same questions that I had originally had when I first began my search for faith so many years before.

My husband did not really know how to respond to my comment. He too was limited only to what I had been sharing with him during this pregnancy. His response was simply that we would deal with that when the time came, and he was right. I had a delivery to focus on, and our future could not move forward until we had accomplished that task. As we completed our conversation, I realized that the contractions had continued to grow in intensity, and we decided it was time to return to our room.

The hours in the day were passing, but there was still much progression needed. Our physician made a second visit after dinner that evening and confirmed that he was pleased with progress thus far. He assured us that when it was time to deliver, things would move quickly, but that we still had a while to go. With no further questions, he again left. I had handled the entire weekend strong. Tasks had kept me busy, and I was holding together fairly well, but I began to grow weary as the evening hours approached. For the first time since our diagnosis, I began to experience fear.

I knew with clarity that my fear was not about the situation or my delivery. I recognized that I had gotten through both the weekend and this difficult day from the strength that came from the many prayers that had been said for me. I knew that my fear was stemming from the thought that the prayers would cease as my friends began to head off to sleep. Immediately, as I recognized why I was feeling afraid, I called my mentor and close friend. I explained to her that I knew that I would not be able to get through this without the strength prayer had given me. I explained that I just needed to know that people were still praying—no matter where I was in the delivery process and no matter what time of night it was. Without hesitation, she assured me that she would make phone calls and she promised me that a prayer team would be in place all night if that was what was needed. Hearing her commit to both praying for me as well as ensuring a team would be praying immediately relieved every bit of fear that I had.

Prior to my phone call to my friend, our physician had indicated that we still had a way to go in our progression. Not that anyone can truly predict labor progression, but we knew he had had plenty of experience and could trust his guidance. We were expecting what could play out to be a long night, but the timing too was all in God's plan. Things changed quickly after my request for prayer and our long expected night turned into only about an hour-and-a-half wait. The moment had literally jumped before us, and we were ready to begin the final phase of labor, pushing. I find it fair to say that prayer trumps even the most dedicated medical experience.

The physician and our nursing team returned quickly to our room following my unexpected request. We had just enough time to get everything set up and everyone in position before the actual delivery would occur. When all was set in place and with my husband by my side, I was instructed to begin pushing. Only a couple of pushes were needed to deliver our precious two-pound-nine-ounce angel that we had long waited for. In an instant, a flood of relief overtook me as the contractions and wave of physical demands on my body subsided, and then silence filled the room. I waited with high hopes that a miraculous cry was going to pierce the calm, but hollow stillness remained.

As reality set in, I looked toward my doctor. He remained at the foot of my bed with his head lowered, cuddling our little one. I had tried to prepare myself for many different scenarios that could have happened in this moment, but never had I envisioned my physician tenderly holding our baby while tears gently drifted from his eyes. I sat for a moment taking this in. He was more than a trained medical professional; he was a man full of compassion and care and was brokenhearted just like us. I took it all in with my husband right beside me. I broke the silence by asking "What is it?" knowing that my faith was riding on his response. I would either celebrate the God that had revealed himself to me and had proven devoutly faithful, or I would return to the question and pain that came with the lifelong void of longing for more. The physician was not aware of what God had revealed to me during this pregnancy, but God used him to complete the story. In response to my question, his gentle, brokenhearted response confirmed God's faithfulness. "It's a girl," he said.

And the tears were relentless. These were not tears of pain, but comfort and confirmation. In that moment, God used my daughter's life to confirm every question I had ever sought answers for. Sweet baby Rose taught me that I can trust in God, with every ounce of my heart. Hebrews 11:1 says, "Now faith is confidence in what we hope for and assurance about what we do not see." I had held fast to hope during this entire trial. I did not know how this story would end. However, in that moment, before I had even held my baby girl, my life felt complete. I knew the heavenly gift that I was given in that moment far exceeded what was being taken from me physically.

The nurse stepped in and took Rose from our physician and placed her in my arms. I looked down at her and felt so much joy. She was absolutely perfect. I caressed her tiny hands and feet, and kissed her puffy little cheeks. As I looked at her, I could see how much she looked like her big brothers. She lay in my arms so peacefully. Her physical body was with me, but I knew she was at home with her heavenly Father. I knew that I would not get to share mother-daughter experiences in this life with her, but even more importantly, I knew that one day I would see her again, and on that day, she would be dancing with me in heaven. Yes, I was sad. I cried a lot. It was the hardest loss of all the losses I had suffered through; but the peace that came with confirmation that God is God in good and bad was so much more powerful. I had chosen to trust in him, and he was faithful. Death had been conquered in the birth of this little angel. I would have to grieve, but this would not be like the past. I would not stuff all of my feelings and bottle up my pain, I had too much to celebrate. Life was just beginning for me. I had honestly come to my knees and asked God for direction. I sought with every bit of my heart and pushed through locked doors to get answers to my faith. It took years of searching, but God did not leave even one of my questions unanswered. He used people and circumstances to guide and direct me in a big way—again, it was to my surprise that I found that he was still not yet finished!

Therefore, if anyone is in Christ,
he is a new creation; the old
has gone, the new has come!
—2 Corinthians 5:17

Chapter **14**

Once Rose was delivered, the staff was full of compassion and love as they gently cared for our sweet baby girl. They dressed her in the pink, rose-embellished outfit that I had chosen and covered her precious head with the baby bonnet. She was so tiny that the two-piece preemie outfit was much too big for her. The bonnet was placed on her head and the top fit perfectly as a full size dress. She looked beautiful. The blessing in this was that I was able to take the bottom portion of the outfit home as a forever reminder of what she wore when we held her. In addition, the hospital provided a photographer for us to capture memories. Packing a camera for our hospital stay had never crossed my mind, but I am so thankful for the photos now.

After spending the first few hours alone with Rose, we chose to have a couple of visitors that night. Our dear friends who had agreed to keep our boys came to visit. Of course, they brought the boys as well. Our three-year-old held his baby sister and whispered "She's sleeping" with a gigantic smile on his face. He had no idea that she was sleeping her eternal rest, but the pride he had in that moment was precious. Our older son was processing things on a different level. We were told that through this, he had asked various questions about God, death, and heaven. He was processing loss in an appropriate and loving way, and growing in his faith through this experience. He chose not to hold his sister, and that was OK. Just being in the room with the three children God had blessed us with gave us precious memories to treasure.

The excitement of holding a wiggly, warm, tiny newborn in the hospital right after a birth is such a fun experience for many, but when the outcome is one as ours was, it is so much more difficult. The experience is not celebrated, and people do not come to visit, but later that night, I longed for one of my dear friends to meet my daughter.

Although I knew that I desired for her to meet my angel, I had not fully prepared my heart for this visit. I had no doubt that she would handle the situation with grace and love, but I found myself completely awestruck as she held my daughter with such sweet love. I could not have been more proud. I knew that my dear friend would not have the chance to come to a soccer game or a dance recital for this little one, so having her there with me, holding my baby was memorable and honoring. Although I had gained many friendships in my search for truth, I realized in that moment how blessed I had been that God had given me this special friend who models such a godly example of love for me.

The next day was filled with more surprises from God. My husband had been in school during our pregnancy. He was supposed to take a final exam for his class; however, he felt leaving me to take the exam was not acceptable. He contacted his professor, who did not agree. My husband was given the option to take the exam or take a poor grade. He opted for the poor grade and stayed at the hospital with our daughter and me. The next day, we again saw how big our God is. My husband received an e-mail that was addressed to the entire class. In the e-mail, the professor apologized for the inconvenience and explained that he had grabbed the wrong briefcase when he left his house (the previous night), and upon arriving at the university to administer the exam, he realized he did not have it with him. The class was excused from the final, and my husband's semester grade did not suffer a single point. God was not only taking care of me during this difficult time but covering my husband as well.

We stayed with Rose for more than twenty-four hours, holding her most of the time. Our tears came in waves, and we did not hold back. I would cry, and then he would cry, but there was never any anger or resentment in our tears. God had used her life to teach us about how big and powerful he really is. God had gotten our attention early on in the pregnancy, and it was our choice to listen. Together, we chose to trust. We did not put an end to the pregnancy when the doctors gave us a way out. We did not give in to panic and despair when days were difficult. We turned to prayer and held fast to hope. Our hope was that our baby would be healed of this condition, but that was because we were limited to what our human minds could comprehend. The truth is, she is eternally healed.

When we finally decided it was time to leave Rose, we were advised by a nurse to walk out of the hospital as a family. She shared that leaving Rose behind would be the most difficult part and encouraged us in saying that having our boys with us as we left would be a start to our healing. I believe she was right. The strength that we felt as we walked out of the hospital as a family was clearly something that simply was not from within ourselves.

The next day continued to introduce new firsts that no parent longs to celebrate. We had to meet with funeral directors to make plans for Rose's final resting place. We had previously made a few contacts from the hospital and had chosen a funeral home that we felt was a good fit for our needs and beliefs. As we entered the facility, we were greeted with compassion and showered with support. Following a gentle welcome, we found that our first decision was to choose Rose's casket. The options were gut-wrenching. The caskets were so tiny; however, still much too big for our little angel. We chose pure white. In addition, we had to choose wording for the ceremony cards, and then we were given an option for the procession. My husband reflected on the fact that we would never get to celebrate her first birthday and that he would not walk her down the aisle or dance with her at her wedding. Knowing this, we chose to have the most beautiful funeral we could to celebrate her life. We decided on having her procession headed by a limo carrying her, and a full procession train leading our friends and family along the funeral route. We left feeling that all of our needs were taken care of well above what we could have ever imagined, but we have learned that God is bigger.

The next stop was the florist to purchase a casket spray. As we drove to the florist, I reflected on how tiny our baby girl was. I felt it would only be appropriate if the spray was filled with roses, but because of her size, I wanted baby roses rather than full-sized ones. I talked with my husband during the drive, and he was in agreement. We arrived at the florist and went inside. The strong aroma of fresh-cut flowers filled the air, and we were immediately greeted at the door. We explained why we were there and what we desired. The florist knew the exact flower we were seeking and escorted us back to the walk-in refrigerator. Her facial expression dropped as she looked around. She excused herself and then returned to us a short while later. Regretfully, she explained that it was prom season and they simply did not have any baby roses available at that time. Emotionally, this crushed me, and I immediately broke down. I believe it was a combination of having held myself together for so long as well as the disappointment from having my heart set on exactly what I felt my daughter deserved. My husband held me for a while and then asked me to go out to the car. He remained inside and tried to handle the floral situation.

Outside, I immediately placed a call to our funeral director. We had had such a positive and professional experience with him, I hoped that he would be able to offer direction, and he did not disappoint. He listened to my heart and provided me with the name of a florist his office used regularly. He assured me that she would be able to take care of our needs. I wrote the phone number down and called his florist immediately after hanging up with him. In that call, the florist promised me they had what I was looking for and gave me directions to her shop. When my husband returned to the car, I did not ask him what took place inside but told him what I found. Without question, he began to make the twenty-minute drive. I felt renewed. It is a baffling situation to live through, knowing that every detail of the celebration you are planning will be the first, the only, and the last celebration you will plan. I just wanted everything to be perfect.

We arrived in the town where the florist was located and began scanning buildings for addresses. The town was older, so the buildings were tall, clothed in broken brick and packed close together. We continued our search for addresses imprinted on doorways and company signs, but in the end, we did not need a numerical address at all. Unexpectedly, my eyes caught the attention of a large mural that had been painted on the side of one of the tall buildings. The painting was a picture of elegant roses with the name of the florist arched above it. The phone number, which matched the number the funeral director had provided me, was also painted on the building. My jaw dropped as I silently read the business name, Rosebud Florist. I could not believe what I was seeing. Perhaps roses are common in the floral world, but I knew that this was just another confirmation that God knew exactly what he was doing. He was covering us and reassuring us that this was his plan, and we were simply chosen to be a part of it. Granted, that did not make this process easy or tear-free by any means, but the comfort that continued to be showered upon us was unbelievable.

Once inside, we met the floral assistant. She had exactly what I had pictured for my daughter—beautiful deep-red baby roses—and the quantity was in surplus. We laid out exactly what we wanted and inserted title banners for "Daughter," "Sister," "Granddaughter," and "Niece." It was beautiful. As we were preparing to leave, my attention was diverted to one more vase. This was already prepared in a stand-alone fridge. This vase was a tall, free-form container sculpted of various hues of purple. It was prepopulated with full-sized roses and had a banner already attached reading, "Sister." Although we had this title on the casket spray, I simply had to have this for my boys to celebrate their sister at the funeral as well. It was the final piece to making Rose's celebration perfect.

With all the planning behind us, we found ourselves at the end of the week, and the funeral was now upon us. It was Friday, only five days after delivering Rose, and exactly one week from hearing the news that our baby had gone to sleep. Emotionally, I felt that I had held up fairly well through the week. I had accomplished the errands and plans that needed to be completed. I had arranged every detail to the best of my ability. I felt as though I had done it with grace and peace, but now I found myself standing alone in front of my closet, facing one final decision that would bring me to my breaking point.

As I prepared for my daughter's celebration, I worked hard to ensure that I had not left out a single element of the plan; however, personal shopping had never crossed my mind. As I stood flipping through blouse after blouse in my closet, I felt myself becoming more withdrawn and empty. It was in that moment, standing alone in my room, that reality struck. After frantically tearing through my limited wardrobe trying on every top and pants I owned, I felt myself weaken as I finally fell to my knees and sobbed. From the pit of my stomach, a volcanic explosion of emotional pain erupted. The tears were uncontrollable, and my body shook as I wailed in agony. Of all the activities that I had successfully accomplished in this most difficult week, I could not achieve the simple task of choosing an outfit to wear to my daughter's funeral. It was all supposed to be perfect. It was supposed to be this wonderful day of celebrating the final chapter to the story that God had been writing, but I couldn't stand up. I lay there again, finding myself alone. I felt the isolation. I was hurting. I was sad. The tears kept coming, and I was unsure if I could find the strength to pull myself together in order to simply take in another breath. But God is bigger.

He met me right where I was. He became the breath in my lungs and the strength I would need. He lifted me up and opened my eyes. In the past, my life was difficult, full of pain and heartache, but this was only because I was looking at the wrong perspective.

As I pulled myself into a sitting position, I realized what God had actually done for me. My story had come full circle, and I realized that not only had my daughter's story been written with a purpose; mine had been too. "'For I know the plans I have for you,' declares the Lord, 'plans to prosper you and not to harm you, plans to give you hope and a future'" (Jeremiah 29:11). This verse became more real to me than it ever had before.

I allowed myself the time I needed, alone in the private corner of my room to grieve. There was no schedule, no task at hand—just me being real. As the tears poured out from within me, I realized how strong I truly had become. Not because I had achieved super powers, or conquered hiding behind deep emotional pain, but because this time, through this loss, Christ was alive in me, and I was willing to see what had always been there.

I didn't write my story, but for many years, I tried to control the outcome. I tried to alter the chapters and hinder any events that would walk me through difficulties. I had convinced myself that I was in charge, and I thought that I knew what I needed, to be successful in this life. However, I found out that the true author of my story actually knew every detail better than I would ever comprehend, and even in knowing all of my pain; he never abandoned me along the way.

God allowed me to search, seek, and question. He allowed me to construct walls around my heart and create avenues that I felt were safe, but thankfully, he did not allow me to stay there. Just as he created and nurtured the delicate blossom of the rose, he also gently nurtured my heart. As I called out to him, he answered, and most importantly, I learned to listen. As our relationship grew, he gently unfolded the intricate layers of pain, lack of trust, and years of feeling alone and abandoned. He knew the plan he had for my life from the very beginning, and even though it took years for me to open my eyes and realize the plan, he never gave up on me. I realize that every prayer I spoke, as well the prayers spoken by others on my behalf, had been heard. He waited patiently for my heart to be ready, for my every question to be answered, and then, just as he changes the seasons, he began to prune me into something beautiful. I know there is still a journey ahead, but it will be an exciting one. Through Christ, I have hope instead of pain, and I find joy instead of mourning. God is good, my friends! He is faithful.

Kathleen Holden is blessed to be married to her best friend, Josh, and lives in the Northern Kentucky area. Together they have accepted the journey of parenting a total of seven children through both biological and adoptive measures. She has served in various aspects of women's and children's ministries as well as hosted small group leadership, which is where she came to know and love Jesus. Kathleen enjoys traveling with her husband and spending time with her children. Her passion to serve others led her to pursue a career in the health-care profession. Kathleen has enjoyed tending to the medical needs of countless patients in various aspects of her nursing career for many years; however, in her search for biblical truth, she knows that her strongest passion is to see lives changed through developing personal relationships with Jesus. She and her family actively support and participate in their church home, Lakeside Christian Church, where they strive to love others daily.